Total Quality for Schools

Other books available from ASQC Quality Press

Quality Education
Gray Rinehart

A Quality System for Education
Stanley J. Spanbauer

A Leader's Journey to Quality
Dana Cound

The Deming Management Method
Mary Walton

Measuring Customer Satisfaction
Bob E. Hayes

To receive a complimentary catalog of publications, call 800-248-1946.

Total Quality for Schools

A Suggestion for American Education

Joseph C. Fields

ASQC Quality Press
Milwaukee, Wisconsin

Total Quality for Schools: A Suggestion for American Education
Joseph C. Fields

Library of Congress Cataloging-in-Publication Data

Fields, Joseph C.
  Total quality for schools: a suggestion for American education/
Joseph C. Fields.
    p. cm.
  Includes bibliographical references and index.
  ISBN 0-87389-206-2
  1. School management and organization—United States. 2. Total
quality management—United States. 3. Education—United States—
Philosophy. 4. Educational change—United States. I. Title.
LB2805.F43 1993
371.2'00973—dc20   93-955
                                                          CIP

© 1993 by ASQC

1098765432

ISBN 0-87389-206-2

Acquisitions Editor: Susan Westergard
Production Editor: Annette Wall
Marketing Administrator: Mark Olson
Set in Times by Linda J. Shepherd.
Cover design by Laura Bober.
Printed and bound by BookCrafters, Inc.

For a free copy of the ASQC Quality Press Publications Catalog, including ASQC membership information, call 800-248-1946.

Printed in the United States of America

Printed on acid-free recycled paper

ASQC
Quality Press
611 East Wisconsin Avenue
Milwaukee, Wisconsin 53202

"The mere formulation of a problem is far more essential than its solution, which may be merely a matter of mathematical or experimental skill. To raise new questions, new possibilities, to regard old problems from a new angle requires creative imagination and marks real advances in science."

Albert Einstein

Contents

Foreword

Quality has become the in-word of the nineties. Surrounded by quality references in the media, advertising, and at professional meetings, educational practitioners and policymakers are trying to find out "What does it mean?" "What does it mean for me?" and "How does it fit with everything else?"

As if sensing this nationwide hunger for information, an avalanche of new publications addressing total quality management and its relationship to America's schools and educational problems has swept down upon us. While I haven't read all of these, those I have seem to fall into one of two groups. Some are written by educators—resonating to quality management's value-based processes, and envisioning possibilities for schools—but who themselves lack direct experience working within a quality-managed work setting. Others have been written by quality professionals—with understanding of the tools and processes—but without deep understanding of the work processes of schools. Few of these latter authors have been able to see schooling as a system of connected work performed by adults attempting to respond to students' needs.

Joe Fields' book stands out from the current crowd, possibly because he has been a worker in both settings. He can draw from both theory and personal experience, avoiding the total quality (TQ) jargon used by quality professionals and first-generation quality immigrants who adopt it without total understanding. As a former teacher, principal, superintendent, and private sector executive, his multifaceted experience is most evident in a unique perspective on the counterproductiveness of national reform programs, as well as his interpretation of W. Edwards Deming's 14 points. Where others take Deming's words and try to add schooling examples, he explores at greater depth the conditions of education that each point addresses.

This clearly written book can push to a greater depth the level of understanding of TQ's potentials in schooling. Ideas are presented *systematically*—always dealing with schools-as-systems within the context of the larger systems of which they are part. As a consequence, the sound, systemic, exponential implementation process it presents makes more sense than the linear processes usually proposed. Within Fields' view, site-based management becomes a stepping stone toward quality schooling rather than an end in itself as currently promoted.

Fields' perspective on the student as "service agent" suggests that school systems seeking to define their "customers" may have an easier job than they think. What if students were their *only* customers, and the others usually identified—parents, higher education, employers, and so on—were, in fact, the student's customers? What type of curriculum and instructional processes would we design and provide if we *really* believed that the student was the only one who could supply what these others customers require? What are the consequences of acting as if it were not true? The answer to this question may be at the heart of restructuring—reorganized school work processes.

Total Quality for Schools: A Suggestion for American Education provides a guide for the quality journey in greater specificity than previously available materials. It is not the final word, because in a continually improving system there is none. It represents but a second or third PDSA (plan-do-study-act) cycle of education thought. Now it must be integrated by the rest of us in subsequent cycles with the experience of the journey itself.

Lewis A. Rhodes
Associate Executive Director,
American Association of
School Administrators

Preface

This book is written for anyone interested in the improvement of American education. Its basic tenet is that the same principles that improve quality services or products worldwide in any human enterprise can be applied to American schools, whether they are preschools or universities. The emphasis here is on the public schools, the backbone of American education equity. The principles referred to have been called total quality management (TQM); here they become the principles of total quality education (TQE).

TQM and TQE embrace the philosophy of the founders of the quality revolution, Walter A. Shewhart and W. Edwards Deming. Both men have been believers in human potential, especially when espoused to group efforts, statistical thinking, long-term planning, and the drive to improve.

This book details methods to identify the conditions for improvement of the schools. It specifies a process for attacking and solving school problems and for gaining the commitment of everyone in the school community. The process has worked in organizations around the world.

Services and producers the world around have implemented the thinking of Shewhart, Deming, J. M. Juran, Philip Crosby, A. V. Feigenbaum, and others. It is the thinking of men like these that has stimulated the people of the Pacific rim to set new rules for their own and others' successes. This new paradigm for using human potential is the basis of this book. This new way of thinking is also the foundation for true human respect and dignity in organizations. Today, cities, hospitals, parks, airlines, delivery services, telephone and electric companies, manufacturers of all kinds, and financial services are but a few of the successful enterprises using the quality approach to improvement.

American educators, like all of us, have lived with their own established paradigms. As professionals they have continually sought the best tools for improving our classrooms and our schools. But like American business, educators have been limited by paradigm patterns for innovation and progress. One such paradigm in education is the intense desire to build education models that intrigue and display the most inspired ideas first, rather than to identify with and deal in the issues and root causes of the American educational emergency.

TQE proposes first to understand clearly the problem at the local level, then match the model. Like TQM, it cannot succeed if deployed from the top, or if it is driven to a compliant work force. Ownership is the coin of the realm in the "Republic of Quality," and unless the people own it, the nation is poor.

Acknowledgments

I am thankful for the many education colleagues, administrators, teachers, custodians, bus drivers, aides, students, and parents who, in my nearly five decades in public education, have believed in the potential of American children. I am especially thankful for those persons who, by modeling exemplary behavior, were an example to me. These folks are too numerous to mention. But I found them in every educational community in which I prospered.

I am especially favored to have lived at a time when America is being revitalized by the thinking of men like Walter Shewhart, W. Edwards Deming, and others working in local schools who are dedicated to improving our schools.

A special note of thanks is due Joanne Artz and Anna Mary Creekmore, who reviewed and improved the manuscript. Dr. John Bugbee, of The Kentucky Center for Excellence in Quality, has been a special friend and kindly critic.

I am especially indebted to my wife, Shirley, and our children for what they sacrificed in this venture. Also, without the opportunity to be involved in private sector total quality management offered by Ross Faires, I would know much less about the subject of total quality. To these special folks and the children of America, I dedicate this book.

Chapter 1
A System for Thinking

"Once one knows how to fix the parts of a car, one would be able to get on with fixing the whole. Once one knows the moves of tennis, one should be able to get on with playing the game. . . . such a principle pervades most of education."

D. N. Perkins

Challenging How We Attack Problems

The state of Vermont is expanding an innovative student achievement assessment technique. Rather than using simple multiple-choice, true-false sets of predetermined questions and answers, all Vermont students in the fourth and eighth grades use the portfolio assessment. State educators say that this portfolio method of collections of student work truly determines a student's ability to think and reason. Vermont education commissioner Richard Mills reports, "Clearly, it works. We find that our students write well, some of them very well. In mathematics they have a long way to go. We concentrated on problem solving and mathematical communications and we found that our students are just not skilled problem solvers."[1] The results of the portfolio tests in Vermont are not unlike the results of the multiple choice tests; Vermont youngsters, like many others, do not have the sophisticated problem-solving skills that workers of the twenty-first century will require. That fact is not new. There are many reasons for this situation, and most of them relate not to the schools but to the attitude toward schools in our society. What is new is that Vermont, like some schools in Pennsylvania, California, New York, Connecticut, and Illinois, is looking at a new method to identify academic problems in the schools.

The portfolio method of testing is not as easy to use as multiple-choice standardized tests. It requires the involvement of parents, teachers, and students. It makes work harder for teachers who must relate more intensely with students. The portfolios are hard to grade. The standards for portfolio grading aren't easily perceived as a simple computer-scored answer sheet. But this approach to education problem solving is affecting the way teachers teach, the way students learn, and the degree to which parents become involved in student learning. In other words, the method used in seeking the problem level of student achievement is as valuable as the instructional strategy used in teaching students academic skills.

These new testing designs are stimulating new teaching techniques partly because teachers, parents, and students are more involved in the "search for the problem." This collaboration and team soul-searching makes a difference. Innovative problem solving is not new to educators; the portfolio method of assessment may be just another try to improve learning. It does suggest, however, that maybe the struggle to attack these problems has merit; the scoring process may be as important as the product scores. Businesses have been learning recently that how they go about the struggle of improvement is important. The Vermont innovation may be saying that school persons may be finding that the how of the learning process may be as important as the learning product.

Are Schools Like Business?

A short conversation with most public school educators will assure us that school learning and teaching is not like business. Teachers will tell you that unlike business, there is little control over the quality of the student sent to school. They will tell you that children just do not come in neat little homogenized bundles ready to be taught. And, although the school instructional and grade advancement provinces may appear to some observers to be similar to a manufacturing process, there is little similarity. School teaching operations are more often customized to individuals. Teachers will admit too that the variety of individual student progress sometimes makes advancement more a formality based on reasons other than achievement.

Additionally, educators will say that the purpose of public schools is to educate all students to their potential, regardless of the obstacles from within or without the schools. And that potential varies too. Educators may suggest that teaching well is more an art than an operation. Educators suggest that the competence required of effective teachers is complex, while the skills needed in business seem stable and easily measurable and obtainable. Educators may believe that business can afford some scrap and rework, and can simply adjust its bottom line. Schools can't afford failures or dropouts.

If there is a similarity between schools and business, school administrators may admit it to be within the realm of fiscal services. Budgeting, purchasing, inventory, accounting, and auditing procedures may be quite similar in education and business. Some administrators may suggest that there is a similarity in personnel recruiting, hiring, and human resource management. The process of finding good teachers, hiring them, and working with them in planning, organizing, and directing the school could be like some businesses. If there is a general similarity between business and education, educators might propose that it exists more in the services sector than in the manufacturing and financial sectors.

Some businesses serve people of all kinds, with multiple services and multiple processes and operations. Such an example could be the business of health care. Hospitals, for example, like schools, receive every manner of person, with every variety of personal health and mental attitude. Emory University reports that, somewhat like the population in the public schools, 75 percent of the people in hospitals are there because of the way they have treated themselves during their lifetime.[2] Generally, patients have been a problem to themselves by refusing to accept and practice reasonable medical knowledge. People cause their own illnesses by smoking, taking drugs, resting irregularly, overeating, and not exercising. People are admitted to the hospital to be healed, with minimum support from home. No matter the kind or condition of the patient, the medical staff does all it can to bring about wellness during a patient's stay. The staff too often learns, however, that the patient will return to the same habits and environment that caused the illness in the first place. A little like schools?

It is difficult for hospitals to contain health care costs and continually invest in new technology. It is a constant challenge to educate patients to share with a professional team the responsibility for their own wellness. It is unrealistic for health care services to be judged only by patient outcomes when so many personal, environmental, and family variables exist. It is a constant challenge to meet patient needs in an ever-changing society.

The specter of rising health care costs, increased regulation, increased sociopsychological distress that promotes physical illnesses, and the public cynicism toward health care givers required the health care industry to find new ways to solve problems and to develop commitment to its patients and to the industry. The first agenda item in seeking improvements was to find a problem-solving process that fit its mission as a business. The second item was the selection of a management style that not only solved problems but expanded commitment. The health care industry has found TQM to be a tool to solve problems. Health care leaders have clearly identified their customers and their customers' requirements, and have improved ways to go about solving health care problems collaboratively.

Schools face several of these same problems. Schools also receive students as people with a variety of mental attitudes and dispositions. Students come to school with little, some, or a lot of preparation to learn; many lack family support, many have it. Some students have poor learning habits, and after strenuous staff support, they return to the same environments and behaviors that fostered poor habits from the beginning. Students come to school expecting to learn, but they do not realize that learning is something like healing—it takes cooperative personal effort.

The rising costs of public education, increased regulation, increased sociopsychological distress promoting discomfort in school, and cynicism toward public school efforts and educators require that Americans seek new ways of solving school problems. It is difficult for schools to contain learning costs and invest in new technology. It is a constant challenge to educate parents and students to share the responsibility of student learning with professional educators. It is unrealistic for schools to be judged only by student outcomes when so many family, community, and state variables impact the school. It is more than a constant challenge to meet the needs of students in an ever-changing society. These kinds of concerns in schools must lead to new ways to solve problems and newer ways to develop commitment in local school communities. American schools need a revitalization of their spirit, a renewal of their value and significance to the nation and the people making them work. But how do we go about it?

First, a Useful Problem-Solving Method

Evidence today suggests that thinking systematically and sequentially may lead to improved understanding, clarity, causes, and solutions of a problem. Some scientists and statisticians have invented procedures for attacking problems and making problem-solving activities more effective. These efforts emphasize tactics such as problem-solving patterns that identify the problem, define the problem more specifically, collect information about the problem, analyze the information, identify alternative solutions, and test one solution at a time.

These tactics encompass sequential, deliberate methods of investigation and solution before problem solvers can leap to conclusions. Although an immediate realistic solution is not guaranteed, these tactics do propose possible answers based on added data. They are not based on subjective hit-and-miss efforts. Research by Alan Schoenfeld has shown that people who use guidelines in solving problems outperform those who do not.[3] People following problem-solving guidelines are able to solve more problems than those without them. People with a problem-solving package also spend less time solving problems.

Successful, high-performance school principals also exhibit this same problem-solving pattern. In a review of dozens of principal candidates in an intensely validated assessment process, those who were judged successful as problem solvers by assessors and their staffs had a plan for solving problems.[4] Each candidate had a set of rules, ready to apply to problems. These rule-of-thumb designs could be used alone or with others. These successful principals relied on tried and true patterns of thought whether the problem was of student discipline, staff evaluation, budget development, or political or public relations.

Unsuccessful candidates lacked such a set of rules. In new problem situations where experience couldn't contribute ready-made solutions, poor-performance principal candidates floundered, seeking answers.

Their best method was a try-anything approach to see if it might work. These participants also had difficulty matching solutions that fit problems. They might be similar to some health care givers who experiment and try remedies without having enough knowledge of the problem, hoping the patient will cure him- or herself or an accidental finding will work. Much evidence exists in nearly every school system to prove that this technique is not new to education.

It seems that skilled problem solvers, whether they be students, scientists, educators, or medical personnel, don't just dive into problems and frantically swim their way to the surface.[5] High-performance problem solvers don't just create answers and try them out. They don't create models without first knowing the problem thoroughly. They think first in terms of some set of guides to help them attack and solve problems.

Several thinkers might offer some guidelines for identifying and committing to resolve problems. D. M. Perkins, in his book *The Mind's Best Work,* offers a several step method to solving problems.[6] From the studies of Seymour Papert,[7] Matthew Lipman,[8] and his own research, all in education, he suggests a long, elaborate sequence to creatively solve problems. First, *be original,* inventing with the end of solution in mind. Second, *find the problem* and explore it thoroughly, looking at all the connotations and alternatives, and then gradually focus on a majority cause. Third, *strive for objectivity* by using as many devices as possible to review the problem. Fourth, *search as necessary and prudent,* exploring alternatives as your resources and time permit. Fifth, *don't expect to be right the first time.* People trade quality for quantity, so determine what degree of perfection you seek and go get it. Expect revision on revision. Sixth, *when stuck, change the problem* so a related problem perspective may end up solving the primary problem. *When confused, employ concrete representations.* Put your ideas on paper. Focus breeds progress, so *practice in context;* keep your efforts in context of the problem. Last, *invent your behavior,* that is, criticize, revise, and devise ways to think about improvements that are important to you.

Perkins' plan works well, but it is individually focused and possibly arduous to implement. The idea is correct, for much of it is part and parcel of how the health care industry is solving its problems worldwide.

Perkins' idea that a problem-solving process is key to improvement is essential to school improvement. But the plan is somewhat difficult to teach and follow, and it lacks a group commitment strategy to ensure that community social and educational problems get solved.

Second, Commit to Solving the Problem

Some problem solvers may short-circuit any problem-solving system to reach conclusions that are "good enough." Educators are used to getting a partial solution to problems; there simply never is enough time, money, people, or effort available to resolve education problems. Herbert Simon's research concludes that people will work to satisfy standards of adequacy.[9] He says that people will work just to beat the previous record or just enough to get the job done. His findings indicate that people usually will not strive to be the ultimate best, just better than the competitor. He says manufacturers will not produce the ultimate best product, just one that will make the customer happy. He calls this "satisficing," searching until an alternative appears to get one just over the top. He believes that this happens because people lack commitment. American health care and American educators seem to deal with a lot of "satisficers" and "satisficing." Satisficing is an attitudinal value.

Quality guru Philip Crosby says that "people create most of their problems through their attitudes."[10] According to Lou Tice, "Attitude is the way you lean . . . either positive or negative . . . and your behavior screams it."[11] In today's world, however, good enough is not good enough. Americans are learning that waste does not have to be a by-product of production; products and services can be defect free. Rework is unnecessary if people do things right the first time. School communities can be committed to excellence, quality, or superior performance in everything including education. Thus, an attitude that leans toward "satisficing"—just good enough—is not acceptable.

Artists and athletes are superior performers because they seek perfection. A person seeking perfection works much harder and examines him- or herself more critically than someone who is attempting to do just good enough. The high-performance athlete does everything necessary to achieve the standard. The high-performance business, health care giver, or education system behaves the same way; it will do everything necessary to reach the standard. In the end, it seems that attitude is what makes the difference between the best and just good enough.

Attitude—this having the heart for it—is what the health care industry and others have found to be the key ingredient to quality improvement. This commitment, the obligation or pledging of oneself to do something in the future, matched with a sound problem-solving method, is improving health care. People in all kinds of roles are involved together in attacking and solving problems and are committing themselves to the problems and to one another. These people are learning that their own interest is served when the interest of all is achieved.

Care givers concerned about quality service call this teamwork. Teams are made up of the patients, families, professionals, and other staff. The patient is an accountable part of the team and the problem-solving process. Whenever possible, the family is involved and also is responsible for the well-being of the patient. In this way, health care givers are solving what once were insurmountable problems. These teams are discovering appropriate solutions after they, together, clearly understand the problem. They do not find answers first; they identify and define the problem first. Through the work of identifying problems and finding solutions, they develop commitment.

Schools Can Do It Too

There is no one best model of this quality improvement for all health care agencies. Each care-giving unit has to identify and solve its own problems. Using the data it has and a simple problem-solving technique to which everyone is committed allows every agency to deliver its own best solution. This same technique might work for schools. If schools can identify a simple problem-solving method and obtain family, student, teacher, administrator, board of education member, and noncertified staff commitment, every school could deliver its own solution, tailored to its local community.

Educators believe they know the answers to teaching and learning problems in the schools. The Edison Project of Whittle

Communications,[12] The Hudson Corporation–America 2000,[13] and the Next Century Schools of RJR Nabisco[14] may give educators the resources to try out some of their ideas. But the all-encompassing questions remain: "How do you get started in a community like this?" "With a staff like this?" "With a board of education like this?" "With students like this?"

As more and more Americans learn about total quality in their workplaces, they understand the need for systematic problem solving, team and individual commitment to improvement, and the value of thinking excellently. Schools can use this momentum of American business and industry quality improvement to their own benefit by linking the terminology, the philosophies, and the management processes in inventing better schools. The total quality management (TQM) process used in private enterprise (but which is moving rapidly into the public sector of state, federal, local, and municipal governments) can be "recycled" to be applicable for the education system. For the sake of our focus, parents, schools, and educators of all kinds whose dedication is to education, we'll call it total quality education (TQE).

TQE is not a business process; it is a people process. It is a process that promotes dignity, self-worth, respect, and adventure for communities of problem solvers. It is a process that builds the human spirit, strengthens bonds between people, and expands the mind of every participant. It is the way educators can fix the parts and the whole. TQE is a simplified education problem-solving process with a reasonable management style.

Some 20 years ago a 16-year-old man named Bill Farris stood in the corridor of a brand new school building in which he had been a student for three months. As a sophomore, he had just enlisted in the U.S. Marine Corps. Some teachers asked him in that corridor, "Why, Bill? Why the Marines? We have a brand new school building, innovative modular schedule, new curriculum, and you won't be participating in it. Why?" Bill, maybe a little more directly than expected, answered, "It's not the school building, it's not the schedule, it's not the curriculum; it's the people in it." He wasn't singling out teachers or one education segment. He saw his role with the Marines as a team player, part of something of excellence. He didn't see his school that way.

Summary

If schools are at all like business, some believe it may be within the fiscal services or human resources areas. But there may be a close similarity between the business of health care and education institutions. Both are unable to specify the quality of client, the conditions of arrival, and the background or environment to which they return.

Schools and health care agencies are currently under pressure of cost containment, additional regulations, expenses of new technology, and the reluctance of clients to be accountable for their own care. Both services are judged by their client outcomes, each existing in environments and personal attitudinal systems that vary greatly. Both are challenged by the constantly changing needs of their clients in an ever-changing, fast-paced society.

A majority of American health care agencies have confronted their difficulties through shared problem solving and deepened commitment on the part of clients and staffs. These agencies are using effective problem-solving techniques that embody specific patterns for identifying and solving problems. Many problem-solving techniques exist; health care givers are using one that involves commitment as well as a pattern for solving problems in teams. They call it TQM.

If the process works for health care, it might work for education. Like many organizations, education must apply an effective problem-solving process and means to commit its publics. TQE embraces the tenets of TQM that concern dignity, respect, and the value of all human potential. The difference is that education communities apply the principles of TQE.

Notes

1. Karen De Witt. "In Vermont Schools, Test on How Well Students Think Draws New Interest." *New York Times,* August 31, 1991, p. 4.

2. R. W. Amber and H. B. Dull. "Closing the Gap: The Burden of Unnecessary Illness." Oxford Press, New York, 1987.

3. Alan H. Schoenfeld. "Presenting a Strategy for Indefinite Integration." *American Mathematics Monthly* (August 1978): 85–88.

4. J. C. Fields. "Problem Solving for Principals." Tennessee Academy for School Leaders Presentation, Memphis, January 1985.

5. D. M. Perkins. *The Mind's Best Work*. Harvard University Press, Cambridge, 1981, pp. 197–198.

6. D. M. Perkins. *The Mind's Best Work*. Harvard University Press, Cambridge, 1981, pp. 214–219.

7. Seymour Papert. *Mindstorms: Children, Computers and Powerful Ideas*. Basic Books, New York, 1980.

8. M. Lipman, A. M. Sharpe, and F. S. Oscanyan. *Philosophy in the Classroom*. Institute for the Advancement of Philosophy for Children, Upper Montclair, N.J., 1977.

9. Herbert Simon. *The Sciences of the Artificial*. Massachusetts Institute of Technology, Cambridge, 1969.

10. P. Crosby. *Quality Is Free*. McGraw-Hill, New York, 1979, p. 211.

11. Lou Tice. "Investments in Excellence." Videotape. The Pacific Institute, Seattle, 1986.

12. W. Raspberry. "The Next Century Schools." *Knoxville News Sentinel*, July 1991, p. 14.

13. U.S. Department of Education. "America 2000: An Education Strategy." Washington, D.C., 1991.

14. W. Raspberry. "The Next Century Schools." *Knoxville News Sentinel*, July 1991, p. 14.

Chapter 2
Beginning Concepts in
Total Quality Management

"Quality is never an accident; it is always the result of intelligent effort. It is the will to produce a superior thing."

John Ruskin

What Is TQM?

TQM in education organizations is the commitment of everyone—parents, teachers, students, aides, servicepersons, board members, administrators, and all others—to meet the requirements of customers, collaboratively. Total (everyone committed) quality (meeting the requirements of customers) management (collaboratively) is the day-to-day belief and behavior of effective TQM organizations. Effective parents, teachers, administrators, and students usually have exhibited not only the definition of TQM but its principles. TQM is not new to high-performance people.

Shewhart used the principles in the 1920s and 1930s in America with Bell Laboratories. Deming applied his own quality principles to the American census of 1941 and to the American war effort of the 1940s. Americans 50 years ago knew only one way—the TQ way. TQM has been a way of life exhibited by high-performance Americans in all of history. High-performance people have committed themselves to ideals greater than themselves and were able to control and discipline their thinking to attain their best in the service to others.

Consider the performance of any winning sports team in the adventure of a game, when every player, every coach, and every water and ball boy or girl is committed collaboratively. They all must think in terms of one another and the team goal: to win the championship. Everyone on the team gives constructive input. Everyone shares in each successful inning or play. Every team member is influenced by the tone and spirit of the crowd watching them; the team responds to the influence of the fans. Even the fans are part of the game and celebrate each success and eventual victory, for as the external customers they are the vital component of TQM. For in sports events as in business or schools the "fans" are paying customers for whom the "team" plays and with whom the "team" wins.

The customer concept is often a token consideration in organizational thinking in public schools. Most educators, when asked to define the customer, generally say "the student." The idea that a customer might be external to the school rather than internal makes sense to some in education. The idea of an external customer being the purpose of education efforts reinforces the importance of a third party in the learning process. It also fixes the focus on the efforts of the school, the teacher, the parent, and the student. The external customer of the school becomes a reason for learning. This third party customer is the organization receiving the school graduate—the company, university, military, or marriage.

If the external customer concept is not considered, the board of education, the state or federal regulatory agency, or the parent will likely assign themselves the role of the significant external customer. They are not the external customer but rather a serviceperson to the customer. Usually what these persons or agencies expect of a school is incompletely communicated if communicated at all. Identification of the clear, specific requirements of the customer are less known. Knowledge of who the customer is and what he or she expects is essential to quality customer service.

Public Education, an Organization

American educators may be reluctant to admit that public schools are organizations much like other organizations. Schools have missions, principles, goals, objectives, leaders, cultures, communication networks, and certain dynamics. Parents supply a resource to which educators apply a variety of processes. These processes include a thirteen-year sequence of assessments to match quality standards to develop a graduate who meets customer requirements. Rework, repair, and sometimes rejection are all a part of the learning-teaching process. It is sad but true that staff effort, parent input, or student work doesn't always pay off in value added to the knowledge acquisition process. Failure is possible and is an expected expense. Sometimes before a graduate can be valuable to an external customer, he or she must be retaught or academically retrained, even after a thirteen-year sequence of similar operations.

The daily operational process in which a student participates is quite similar to that of all other students in one day in one school. Schools maintain a similar organizational process in the quest of individual outputs. It is the same, organizationally, for one student or five hundred students for 13 years of school days. The beginning of a youngster's day exemplifies this. Is there much difference, operationally, between business and education organizations? Note the flow chart of operations for one child shown in Figure 2.1. Check the many operations, processes, monitorings, quality checks, and assessments that occur in the beginning and first periods and probably the rest of a normal school day. Consider, too, that these processes vary somewhat for every child.

Public school organizations not only mirror other organizations in their processing of services, but they depend, like other organizations, on cooperation from many populations supplying them with resources. Like health care agencies, they must gain cooperation to maximize successful efforts in serving others. In order to be a most successful school, a school organization tries to regulate the behaviors of children, provide uniform learning materials, standardize expectations of parents, and sometimes homogenize the instructional strategies of staff. The operational procedures are uniform to ensure equitable inputs of all resources. Procedures are designed to afford equal opportunity for all achievers. Is not this somewhat like a business process?

The obstacle the school contends with daily from many publics can be called variation. Variations are simply differences. Every aspect of schooling deals with differences in children, differences in parents and parental support, differences in teachers, and differences in continuous curricula and learning resources. If schools could reduce variation in

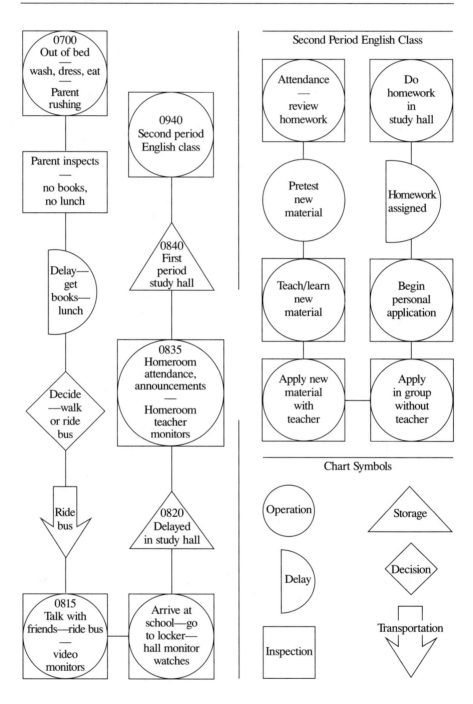

Figure 2.1   Flow Chart of Some Daily Processes of Middle School Student

inputs, they would not have to regulate as stringently. They would improve and succeed more readily in producing quality graduates.

How can schools begin to reduce this variation? Effective businesses use the TQ approach. They agree first on who their target customer is and what his or her requirements are, the business purpose, the requirements of the suppliers of resources, and their business management style and its operational processes. To apply TQ to schools, we must also start with the customer. Who is the customer of schools?

A Common Problem

Public schools are not unlike public infrastructures. Hospitals, utility services, roads, police, and fire protection all suffer similar maladies; they have difficulty prioritizing their customer. Yes, each infrastructure service is applying new technology; some are attempting quality initiatives; and sure, many of our systems work better than those in other countries. But customer perception is their moment of truth. When a power company stops transmitting energy to computers that control airline schedules, and passengers miss flights or duties because of one power company employee's thoughtlessness, all company reputations suffer. When Americans feel they must arm themselves with weapons or drive four-wheel-drive vehicles in case of road problems, public service reputation suffers.

The requirements of Americans as customers have changed with the new economy. Americans now choose from 572 models of cars, vans, and trucks. Consumer banking has now changed from a usual six to more than a hundred services. Supermarkets have doubled the number of items available from 12,000 to 24,000 in 10 years.[1]

American customers expect delivery of pizzas and airplane rides to be on time, every time. They believe they have the right, rather than the privilege, to choose from products and services from an international array of designs and flexible limitation. Americans are looking for convenience. Whether we are talking user-friendly, one-stop shopping, or drive-in quick service, Americans want it now.

As new-age customers, Americans are expecting the same service quality in the public sector that is becoming readily available in the private sector. Americans do not expect to pay to stay sick. They do not expect to pay for interrupted utility services. They do not want to have to personally secure themselves, their families, and their homes and pay for public services too. People do not want to pay twice through taxes and purchases for any public service, including education. Customer behaviors have been driven by the available quality attraction to the customer's own requirements. Americans are learning that things can be done right, and the right things can be done. Services and products can be durable. Services they buy or pay for can work right the first time and ever after. There is a worldwide revolution against shoddy workmanship, craftless services, and mass mediocrity, whether we wish to believe it or not. American customers are changing faster than the organizations serving them. Thus the American customer is more sophisticated than ever, and this sophistication affects his or her expectations of the schools as well as other public or private infrastructures. Schools suffer the results of this new consumer expectation of the economy, just as other infrastructures suffer under these expectations.

The Information Age Makes Quality Education Vital

Because we are now driven by an economy where information is more valuable or at least as valuable as capital, knowledge really is power. People with information can invent or apply technology; technology produces better services and products, and this creates competitive leadership and capital. The three sources of business success worldwide—information, technology, and capital—are led by information.[2] Education is the tool of learning; it is the foundation for collecting information. Education is the tool to think differently, to achieve excellence, to set the boundaries of world competition. Education is the continuous improvement of thought.

Today other countries are sending their children off to the finest schools in the world. Some third world countries are making the education of their work forces their top priority. Currently, India is exporting medical practitioners, scientists, economists, and engineers. Japan is opening financial service institutions worldwide. Korea is challenging the world in manufacturing and electronics. Many foreign countries have learned that information pays in customer satisfaction. Customer satisfaction pays in employed work forces. Employed work forces in any country enjoy higher standards of living and increased job opportunities in the future for all people. American children are competing now with progressively educated work forces for jobs all over the world, as well as in America.

Quality products and services are the result of information access. Information access is the result of education. If America is interested in continuing to attract the world's business, it must strengthen its public education services. The signs of information decay are rampant in American communities; jobs that used to be native are now in foreign countries. Good jobs in America are often taken by foreigners. Being open for business now means being open to employee candidates with the best education. Strengthening educational services means a quality revitalization in the schools that simply means no unhappy customers— as consumers or learners.

Neither Chicken Nor Egg

American education serves the individual as a contributor to American culture, the American political system, and the American economic system. All three—cultural, political, and economic systems—are America. Educators must confront this age-old question of whom to serve (the individual or the state) and resolve this question in favor of the customer and the American culture, political system, and economic system.

This triad, American culture, political system, and economic system, must become the external focus of schools. Schools must contribute to the continuation of American culture, the American political system, and the American free enterprise system. Youngsters need to be taught to be contributors to this triad. Upon graduation, youngsters must be able to serve others with whom they will cooperatively stimulate the progress and growth of our country. Educators must confront the question of "whom to serve, the individual or the nation," and resolve this question in favor of the external customer, the people of our nation.

Usual American reasoning considers the parent or student as the customer. This attitude is based on the following kind of thinking: "As a parent, I believe that the school has a responsibility to educate my child. The school should teach effectively what I believe, in a disciplined format. It should be responsible for my child when I am not with him or her." This is a parent-as-external-customer focus, and it tends to make the teacher responsible for learning and puts the student in the position of being right without being responsible. It puts school boards and administrators in constant mediatorship roles between parents, students, and instructors. It results in problems with which educators are unable to deal, some of which are contrary to good learning and teaching environments.

State and Federal Education agencies and school boards of education often require educators to serve themselves first. The duties performed by educators for bureaucratic purposes often have little to do with the direct education of the child or direct service to the employer or post-secondary school receiving the graduate. Time and effort spent serving state and federal agencies is time and effort lost for important internal or external customers. Requirements of these agencies confuse educators as to "who is the customer." This confusion results in diffused efforts to children and external customers. It is important that there be school-wide, or system-wide, consensus about who the priority customers are and what priority of effort must be given them.

What parents expect may be contrary to policy. What education boards expect may be contrary to parent expectations. What teachers know as sound learning theory may be contrary to both board and parent expectations. So teachers spend much of their time in the half-a-loaf-is-better-than-none syndrome, doing things right or doing the right things only half of the time. It seems that only in strong homogeneous communities is this dilemma resolved favorably.

The practice of perceiving the student as customer affects student performance and preparation. Students do not know or cannot usually verbalize their requirements as customers of the school. Without a clear, cooperative problem-solving effort, the investigations of parent, teacher, board, and administration for students may have unclear results. This resulting set of customer requirements may actually be inconsistent with the needs of the student as service agent of the future. The requirements may not fit him or her to a work force, a university, the military, or a marriage.

Who Is the Customer?

School leaders recognize the importance of clear mission statements, guiding principles, and goals and objectives for effective school organizations. Local principals realize that leadership requires every staff member to have his or her own vision, and they often frame these statements and display them on their walls. The president of the United States has determined some national goals with governors and others.[3] State legislatures require one- to five-year plans of education boards which detail goals and objectives and plans for their achievement. Part of the value of these efforts is to support a more synchronous organization of parents, teachers, students, and all others in the pursuit of excellence in education.

One organizational arena essential to success is a component called customer focus strategy. Customer focus strategy answers the following questions:

- Who is the customer?
- What strategies do we use to identify him or her?
- What are his or her requirements?
- How do we respond to his or her requirements?
- How do we communicate continually with him or her to ensure continued response to his or her needs?

A TQ customer focus strategy is based on behaviors that indicate there are external and internal customers. External customers are those served outside the organization. Internal customers are those served inside the organization. In either case, Stew Leonard's customer rules apply.[4]

Rule number one—The customer is always right.

Rule number two—If you ever think the customer is wrong, refer to rule number one.

Let's first consider education's external customers.

The organization receiving the student is *the customer.* The organization will be the community and may be a university, a business, the military, a government service, or a marriage. It may follow that after graduation the student will become a "service agent" to a receiving organization. This changes the role of parent to be one of a "vendor" of precious, incomparable resources to teachers. It then follows that teachers become developmental specialists of the "service agents." In this brief sequence, each party serves someone in favor of serving education's external customer.

This sequence of service possibly promotes attitudes and behaviors that reinforce each other and lead to collaboration throughout the organization. Persons with school roles might become co-responsible in serving an external customer's requirements. Quality schooling becomes defined in terms of the expectations of the external customer and becomes measurable in terms of the co-responsibility of all the school participants. It may become more likely that parents, guardians, human service agencies, teachers, and others might perceive their roles more clearly in light of everyone's duties to meet the external customer requirements rather than their own personal interests.

From the student's point of view of him- or herself as service agent preparing to serve an external customer, he or she may feel responsible for his or her own learning and preparation to serve others. After all, neither parent, teacher, administrator, education board, nor coach serves the external customer directly; only the student has this responsibility. The more the student is involved in sharing the purpose of schooling, the more ownership he or she develops for his or her own learning. The student also gathers more ability as a future service agent. Being more fully accountable for him- or herself, the student may strive to gain more knowledge and more skills. Basically, learning might become a student initiative, driven by the student in preparation for being the graduate who serves the customer.

Teachers might become facilitators, advisors on request, accessors to knowledge. Parents learn that they must provide the best ready-to-learn student possible. Administrators learn that their role is to remove obstacles to learning. Accountability for external customer satisfaction is focused on specific, known responsibilities not only for the student but for everyone serving each other in the organization. Clear external requirements bring focus to all efforts in the schools. It is hoped that what declines is the self-interest of all populations in the school community. Everyone focuses on the needs of the external customer in light of his or her responsibilities.

Internal Customership

In some jurisdictions, the teacher is customer. Parents and students behave to please the teacher and to meet the teacher's requirements. In some places the school board is customer, and all efforts—conscious and unconscious—are directed to individual or collective satisfaction of a selected or elected school board member. In each of these examples, a figurehead external customer supplants the consumer organization as the true external customer. If this figurehead customer is aligned with the true external customer, all is well. If it is not, all is fruitless.

Internal customership works like this: Every parent, teacher, student, administrator, coach, custodian, diagnostician, nurse, cook, bus driver, and board member accepts his or her responsibility for serving others in a chain of internal customers who serve the graduate who serves the external customer with skills that satisfy requirements. Everyone depends on someone else to ensure his or her own success. Everyone's success depends on the kind of resources, services, and goods he or she is provided to meet his or her own internal customer requirements. Responsibility for success of the chain depends on the service to and from each link.

In the perspective of customership, all players within the school community can become internal customers in the development of the high-performance service agent. Each internal customer serves another specifically and personally to satisfy the needs each internal customer requires to serve the next internal customer, thereby contributing to the final graduating service agent. Each person in the school community says to his or her internal customer, "What is it I can do for you? Here is what you can do for me so that I can serve you better."[5] Ultimately this collaboration achieves external customer satisfaction. As individuals achieve internal requirements, internal and external quality comes alive. Customer requirements are being met.

Internal customership begins with the board of education making available the human and physical resources needed to satisfy its own internal customers. Much like a business board of directors, the board of education's responsibility is to create the resources to satisfy internal customer requirements so that external customer requirements are satisfied. These probably include learning environment services such as management, purchasing, transportation, inventory, and supply of goods and materials, as well as methods and processes. Who are the internal customers? To the board they are the custodians, the maintenance persons, and the administrators who are responsible for providing goods and services to their own internal customers, the teachers.

Teachers are also the internal customers of parents. Parents are responsible for providing the highest level of student possible to teachers. The parent as supplier should supply children prepared to inquire, acquire, and require of the school on a daily basis. The teachers' sole internal customer is the child. The level of internal customer satisfaction of student requirements depends on the fulfillment of a teacher's internal customer requirements from the initial responsibility of the board to the responsibility of the service agent graduate. The child's short- and long-term educational customer is his or her employer, college, marriage partner, community, career, and lifetime.

Figure 2.2 shows the education customership cycle. The cycle represents the continual flow of service from community to board of education to administrative servers to teachers to student service agents. Notice that parent services and external human and youth services join the cycle at the teacher link. Consider that weak or strong links in the cycle will make a significant difference in the quality of student as service agent to the community.

Summary

TQM is everyone being committed to meeting the requirements of customers. It is not new. High-performance educators traditionally have used the principles of TQ. Shewhart, Deming, and others have shown that the principles have worked in business and wherever human organizations flourish. Schools are organizations and do the same things all other active organizations do. They diagnose, apply resources, and review and apply operations and quality assurance assessments. They have customers to serve and requirements to meet.

The American customer and economy have changed. Today's customer has higher expectations of variety, timeliness, durability, choice, and convenience. Value is important to the customer, and the customer decides what value is. Today's economy is driven by information, technology, and capital, all of which depend on education. Today the customer is in the driver's seat internationally in a market where customer requirements will be satisfied. What is often lacking in public service is a customer focus strategy which determines who the external and internal customer is, what he or she expects, and how the service will respond to the customer to meet his or her requirements.

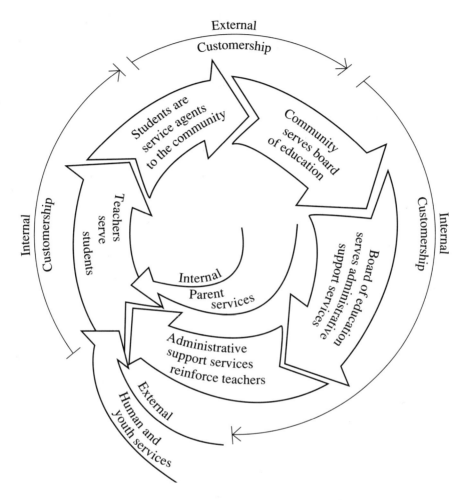

Figure 2.2   The Educational Customership Cycle

Schools must decide who their external customers and internal customers are and what their requirements are. The many shareholders in the school business often cloud the customer issue, making it difficult to define the external customer and the internal customer. Once customers and requirements are clarified, the definition of improvement may be confirmed.

Notes

1. American Society for Training and Development. "The New American Economy." *Training* (November 1989): 2.

2. M. Fitzgerald. "Highly Educated, Multi-Skilled People." Tacoma Education Association Presentation, Washington State Economic Development Board, Tacoma, 1988.

3. U.S. Department of Education. "America 2000: An Education Strategy." Washington, D.C., 1991, p. 19.

4. Tom Peters. "In Search of Excellence." Public Broadcasting System Presentation, Boston, 1988.

5. C. Philip Alexander. "Who Is Your Customer?" Communiqué of the Human Resources Division. Milwaukee: ASQC, Vol. 6, No. 3 (September 1990).

Chapter 3
Shewhart Problem Solving
and Education

"Research is a high hat word that scares a lot of people. It needn't. It is nothing but a state of mind. It is the problem solving mind instead of the let-well-enough-alone mind."

Charles Kettering

Schools and a State of Control

Quality craftsmanship has always been determined by the customer's willingness to purchase or use a product or service. Until mass production, quality was built into products and services one at a time by one craftsman, from supplies from single suppliers. This assured quality products that satisfied customers. Often the article was customized for the customer according to his or her requirements.

Similar things happened in learning. A young person was apprenticed to a master and was taught to satisfy a significant third party, the customer. This philosophy of excellence hasn't changed; TQ then and now is meeting the requirements of the customer.

The customer is still a consumer, but now there are more and different kinds of them. The number of craftsmen, the number of segmented processes, the number of inconsistent operations, and the number of suppliers have changed in modern business and schools. This consideration raises a question of the reality of a TQ school. How can schools create a TQ graduate with so many people, processes, and operations involved? Schools can hardly handle all their present responsibilities, problems, publics, and policies.

The answer to this question comes from the results of investigation into TQ theory and its applications. TQ theory suggests that the processes involved in schooling or learning may be "out of control." According to Shewhart's premise, there is too much variation in the process. Variation is a change in data caused by influences within or without the system. In schools, much of this variation is caused by continuous interference from within and without the school system.

Public schooling has many stakeholders, parties who have interest and input to the process. Among these are parents, teacher unions, state, federal, and local policymakers, administrators, health service agencies, chambers of commerce, higher education institutions, local community groups, and students, to name some. Each in its own way attempts to control the process of education, thus causing more variation. Deming might call this behavior tampering. Each group or party in its own way spends its effort attempting to put the process into its own control using subjective, individualized efforts.

While each group is affecting the educational process, it is causing disorder to other parts of the process. This tampering often causes out of control operations to pop up elsewhere. Sometimes the simplest attempts to make things better come from little data supporting change. For example, sometimes the simplest reason causes change in the schools. How often is it said by parents or teachers, "Other schools do it in the fifth grade. Why can't we?" "Other teachers do this, we should too." "Well, we had that planned in our curriculum, but we had to spend our time on . . ." "If we had only known about this in the beginning of the day, the month, the year . . ." Subjective tampering with little prepared data or research has created school organizations where all the fans have become the coaches.

While an administrative individual or school group is trying to put the process under control, someone else from a state department may be mandating a new attendance policy or a new resolution to saving "at risk kids," or changing the school schedule to fit new pressures. Even these additional strategies designed to improve the schools are too often designed on intuition rather than real data or measured knowledge of what the school process is already doing. In some schools the teacher simply closes the classroom door and hopes to be left alone. The resolution of this problem of variations is truly an awesome challenge.

At other levels of the education hierarchy, at the state, federal, or higher education levels, things aren't much better. Where the state and federal governments should focus on issues such as education equity for all, adequate funding for the education emergency, and managing their own commitment to support local education, they are caught in a paper-shuffling bureaucracy that uses precious tax dollars to maintain itself—tax dollars that should be spent on children. State and federal education leaders, driven by personal and political self-interest, tamper with the ideals, policies, and regulations that are driven down to the schools, causing all the more variation and "out of control" processes. Higher education isn't much better. Colleges of Education, in their zeal to disseminate new theories and practices, frequently intervene in the public schools. This intervention comes about through college instructor manipulation of undergraduate and graduate education students, who are encouraged to experiment with college instructor ideals in the public schools. Many of these ivory tower ideas are not practiced in the college, but only in the students' schools. College of Education tampering isn't with their own anti-quated, provincial, self-centered system but with the public schools, who don't need any more variation from outside interference.

In all levels of the educational hierarchy there is no consistent manner of solving problems, no sequence of activity for improving education, no ongoing pattern for entering suggestions, and no consistent use of measures that could help evaluate school programs or revise them. Consider curriculum change in schools, for example. The curriculum in schools can be changed by any one of many methods. The state may mandate it. The local board of education may require it due to the insistence of one board member or one interested parent or parent or teacher group. It may be changed by educators who may carry new curriculum ideas to a "curriculum council," often a teacher master agreement structure contracted to ensure teacher input into curriculum change. Additionally, teachers may change the curriculum within their classrooms as they deem necessary, singularly or as a concerned group. Once a curriculum idea is implemented, often there is too little monitoring of its outcome. Sometimes it is not even recorded for other teachers or next year's teachers to continue.

Enter Shewhart and Deming

These schooling problems are no less perplexing than those faced by Shewhart at the Bell Telephone Laboratories in the 1920s and 1930s, or those faced by Deming in Japan in the 1950s. Shewhart was expected to provide solutions to the production and distribution of telephones and the networking of telephone lines in a country ready to grow. Deming was asked by the Japanese to show them how to get out of the routine of making junk products in a country that had no resources and that was financially deficient. Both men succeeded.

Shewhart became the pioneer philosopher-statistician who produced affordable, dependable communication links throughout America at a profit. Today's telephone communications system is a tribute to quality improvement theories resulting in control based on the use of data. Deming, a student of Shewhart, became the quality philosopher whose theories launched a nation steeped in negative self-worth to one of the wealthiest in the world. Deming emphasized quality aimed at the needs of the customer, with an eye to the vended supplies used to produce goods and services. All of this, he emphasizes, can improve with management commitment to concentrate on people as the most important resource. Japan's success is a tribute to Deming thought.

The Mind of Walter Shewhart

Shewhart based his theories on inductive rather than deductive approaches to thinking. "Inductive thinking may be explained as a method of reasoning or proof in which a conclusion is reached about a problem or process by examining a valid sample of the observed problem. Inductive thinking goes from the unknown to the known; having nothing and finding something from which to begin."[1] Inductive goes from an idea to information to prediction based on the information. Deductive thinking is the method of reasoning for reaching a conclusion from a premise or principle, from the known to the unknown. Coaches use inductive thinking when they know nothing about the competing team. They send scouts out to acquire information and then use this information to predict what the competitor will do in the game. Coaches use deductive thinking when they have great knowledge of their own players and formulate game plays based on that knowledge.

Shewhart's thinking is somewhat like the scientific method, but in quality terms. Scientifically, one would make a hypothesis, conduct an experiment relative to the hypothesis, observe what happens in the experiment, collect data from the efforts, and test the hypothesis again to assure the results were consistent. Shewhart perceived improvement as a continuing cyclical effort based on *planning a change,* which includes identifying and defining the problem (a ninth-grade attendance problem in winter, for example), investigating the problem by collecting valid data from a sample (a valid cross-section of ninth-graders), and analyzing the data to identify causes and solutions. (Just what do these data tell us about ninth-graders and attendance in winter?) Shewhart's second step is then to do something about a solution. Select a best solution and *carry it out (do)* on a small scale (ninth-graders seem susceptible to the flu, so let's try fogging some rooms twice a day). *Study,* the next step, is to observe the results from the proposed solution, collect data (possibly using the same grade and method of investigation first chosen), and study the results. Find out what old and new information is available. (What did we learn about this attendance problem?) Then *act:* adopt the change that seems a probable solution, or abandon it or run it through again under a different environment. Then *plan:* begin the cycle again with renewed effort or broaden the effort and continue the cycle until the attendance problem is resolved. This is known as the Shewhart cycle—a plan-do-study-act (PDSA) cycle (Figure 3.1). Start at the number 1, through 2, to 3, to 4, and then again to 1. Application of this cycle will ensure thorough consideration of problems and solutions.

The Shewhart cycle can be an individual or participatory effort with improvement and service of customers as the single focus. Schools might use the PDSA cycle and focus on the requirements of internal and external customers as part of a TQM effort. The first two components of quality improvement are commitment to meet the customer's requirements and commitment to attack and solve problems in a consistent method to meet the customer's requirements.

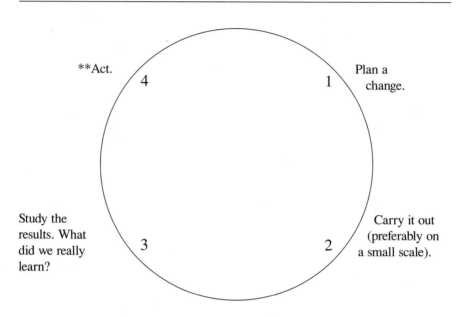

**Act. Adopt the change. Abandon it. Run through it
again, possibly under different environmental conditions.

Figure 3.1   The Shewhart Cycle

Shewhart's cycle reflects the scientific method, but it is also the
result of his following beliefs:[2]

1. The future can be predicted from the terms of the past.

2. The future is preordained by the present or the past unless there
   is interference.

3. We use past experiences inefficiently because they are not sys-
   tematized into rules.

4. We can control the future if we identify and use limits of control.

5. We can control processes if we know the processes objectively.

6. We fail to use many known and unknown rules of nature in our
   favor.

In the case of ninth-grade attendance problems, curriculum change,
state or federal policy deployment, or higher education experimenta-

tion, schools will continue to be the result of their pasts unless we use the information of the past to intervene. Educators can control the future by knowing the past and present processes objectively. There are rules of reason to help us if we learn and use them.

Basics of All Knowledge

Shewhart's thinking to this point suggests that from a small amount of valid data we can infer predictable outcomes and possibly predict solutions. If we know the problem objectively, through collected measurements and the use of the rules of probability and statistics, we can predict the future.[3] We can also control the problems of the future. The PDSA cycle is application of the theory, using data and data interpretation to control processes. This type of reasoning will require discipline, hard work, and group commitment and study, all of which may be absent in some parts of our school community—Americans are rather independent individuals. But we must persist.

Parents, school boards, and others in education sometimes want instant solutions, and that's part of the problem. Too often solutions are applied without thoroughly knowing the problem, or the symptom of the problem rather than the problem itself is attacked. Solutions are sometimes applied that have little to do with the problem. Many education improvement specialists have given up hope in the ability of many parents to support their own children's learning. Rather than focus on and seek improvement in parental accountability for children, these specialists have just added more programs to the schools targeting these "at risk" children. What about the accountability of their parents?

Quality improvement the Shewhart way is not easy, but the reward for dedication to inductive thinking and statistical reasoning is exciting. Participants using inductive thinking and statistical reasoning find that a deeper understanding occurs of the natural order of the world and what we are doing in it. This new knowledge is not just of Shewhart's inductive thinking, his beliefs, and the Shewhart cycle, but the basics of a lot of new knowledge school communities may have seldom considered seriously. A summary of this knowledge could be, "The future of any process unfolds to the observer through continuous study and collection of objective

information about the processes. You can tell the future from the past."
That is not new to people, but the manner in which we find and
analyze the past is new to many people in education. Shewhart says it
in these words:

> "There are three important components of knowledge, (a) the
> data of experience in which the process of knowing begins,
> (b) the prediction p in terms of data that one would expect
> to get if he were to perform certain experiments in the
> future, and (c) the degree of belief pb in the prediction p
> based on the original data or some summary . . . as evi-
> dence e . . . knowledge begins in the original data and ends
> in the data predicted, these future data constituting the
> operationally verifiable meaning of the original data." [4]

For educators this means many things, among them that decision
making without data or objective information of the school process or
problem is probably futile.

Locally political or governmentally distant decisions about schools
may be more interference than intervention. Consider the overall
impact, for example, of the Handicapped Youth Act relative to main-
streaming in the classroom and maintenance of high learning expectations of every child. Initially, in an effort to help physically and
mentally handicapped children, Congress mandated teachers and
schools, already understaffed and underresourced, to specialize efforts
to teach handicapped children in the regular classroom without training the teachers or providing resources for the teachers responsible for
implementation of the law. This is a classic example of federal tampering without thorough knowledge or information about the school and
its conditions. It also shows the confusion at the federal and sometimes
state levels of the responsibility to support local education rather than
deploy policies without the dollars needed to implement government
policies fully. The first implementation of the Handicapped Youth Act
seemed to be another solution without thorough knowledge of the
whole problem. Resources reached teachers in this case long after their
frustration with the problem had peaked.

Shewhart practiced what most educators wish could be done in
schools. Educators, like Shewhart, know that taking action on a

process without knowledge of its state of control is probably damaging to the process. Today, more than ever, outsiders are tampering with the education process, causing more variation. In order to prevent unwarranted interference or intervention, Shewhart introduced statistical problem solving in the form of run charts and control charts.

Run and Control Charts

Shewhart's fundamental statistical theory requires us to identify something measurable in a consistent process, collect the data through observation or measures, and record the data on a lined chart. By constructing a chart and applying the data, we can examine the data and observe what the process is doing over a period of time. We can see the high points of the process, the frequency, and the extent of changes in the problem's process; we can determine *why* the process is acting the way it is. The *why* may be "common causes," causes of variation that are inherent over time, affecting every outcome and everyone working in the process. They are part of the "system" being measured as designed by federal and state governments, higher education institutions, school boards, teachers, parents, aides, students, or others involved in the process. A school board policy about student bus transportation schedules is part of the "system," inherent to the process of schooling; it can be a common cause. Secondary school student schedules as required by the school teaching staff may be a common cause inherent to the process being measured.

Causes of variation that arise because of circumstances that are not inherent to the process may be considered "special causes." A special cause lies outside the process being measured. If a classroom process is being measured, then school administrator interference may be a special cause. If the school system process is being measured then a day where all normal school activities are cancelled may be a special cause.

Let's apply this quantifying of data to develop a run chart. A run chart is a chart of plotted statistical data of a series of random samples over a period of time, for example, winter fourth-grader absences, fifth-grade parent-teacher contacts per month, homework completed each month, dollars expended per pupil per district per year, or student-teacher ratio per state, per year. Random samples of data from each of these topics represent the process in some kind of observable form with actual data.

Suppose some teachers believed that parent-teacher contact was a problem in their school. They decided that sixth-grade teachers would measure and record the number of daily parent-teacher contacts through use of the PDSA cycle. Data collected every day for four weeks would give them enough valid information. Each sixth-grade teacher would collect on a checklist the number of parent contacts that occurred to him or her daily during the four-week period. The chart would indicate the days of the week and the four weeks on the base from left to right: Monday, Tuesday, Wednesday, Thursday, Friday, Monday, Tuesday, etc., for four weeks. The number of contacts per day (up to 10 contacts per day) from one at the bottom to ten at the top, would be on the left vertical side. By placing a dot in the graph square immediately above the day of the week and to the right of the number of contacts, each teacher will have developed a run chart. By connecting the dots sequentially from left to right (Monday, Tuesday, Wednesday, etc.), the teacher will have created a picture of the process, or a graph.

If all sixth-grade teachers added their data together for each day of the four weeks, they might represent it on a run chart like the one shown in Figure 3.2. By connecting the dots, they develop a graph.

This chart is a record of the past. From it a group of teachers can observe how the parent-teacher contact process has been working. Teachers have quantified the process of parent-teacher contact. The run chart displays the total number of contacts, frequency of contacts, and particular days of contact. They now have information to determine whether contacts are low, high, or moderate. They may discover that Mondays are high contact days, mid-week contacts are low, and Fridays are heavy contact days. In addition to collecting data about their problem, they may have information for other problems also. Would this be a useful tool for determining when to close the school for parent-teacher conferences? Do the data give us other suggestions for solutions to try in the PDSA cycle?

The run chart is the parent-teacher contact process in record. It may reflect parent contacts for the whole year, although additional investigation may be needed. It certainly reflects parent contacts in the

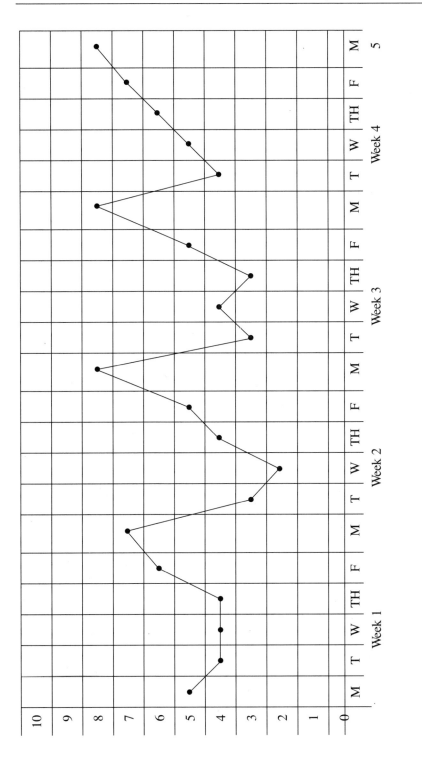

Figure 3.2 Run Chart for Parent-Teacher Contacts

sixth grade for four weeks. This chart can be used to look for patterns, solutions, or more information. It might be a part of a presentation to administration or to the Parent Teacher Organization in order to request solutions. At the least, it helps educators understand the parent-teacher contact process.

A control chart is a run chart with statistically determined upper and lower limits or levels charted above and below the process average. These upper and lower limits are calculated from statistical techniques, not just experience or administrator expectations or board policy. These limits (standard deviations, or measures of variation) are determined by allowing a process to occur, measuring and collecting data from it (such as in the run chart), using a mathematical formula to determine limits, and then charting the data, the limits, and the process average. The mathematical formula for determining the limits of the process provides an economic balance between searching too much for special causes when there aren't any and not searching when there are some to be found. A process can best be improved when we have eliminated all the special causes (causes of variation that arise because of specific circumstances) and the process is in statistical control.

Statistical control simply means a stable process, one with no indication of any special causes of variation. The behavior of the process in the near future is predictable. The process may still have acting upon it common causes that are the responsibility of the board and administration. Once the process is under control, that is, special causes are effectively eliminated, control charts can be used continually to monitor the process and begin improvement.

Control charts are representations of data reflected against a model statistical picture called the normal distribution curve. Educators call it the bell curve. The curve represents a normal distribution of frequencies. One hundred random measurements of any stable recurring process could look like the bell curve if the kind of action and number of occurrences of that action were plotted, and if there were no special causes.

If we were to measure the height of 100 randomly selected male high school basketball players, we would find that there are small frequencies of certain height ranges at both ends of the curve and large

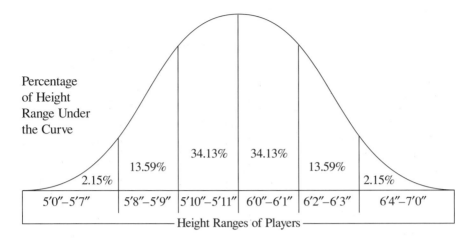

**Figure 3.3 Bell Curve Representation of the Height of
100 High School Basketball Players**

frequencies of certain height ranges in the middle. This distribution, charted, would look like the chart in Figure 3.3.

PDSA Cycle and Charts in the Schools

Let's try an example in the schools using a common high school teacher concern: "I never have enough time to teach students." Five ninth- and tenth-grade teachers who feel this way get together to discuss the problem. Using the PDSA cycle and the *plan* component, they decide that the problem is interference in classroom instructional time. They further define it to include several kinds of interference—administrative, student, and other.

The teachers create a checksheet to record information from five teachers from five different periods for five days. They list the possible causes by brainstorming down the left side of the sheet. They identify the days as day 1, day 2, day 3, and so on, across the top of the sheet. The day is then broken into periods immediately below the word *day,* and each period—1, 2, 3, 4, and 5—is listed for each day. Vertical columns are used to allow them to place a check mark under the day and period to the right of the cause to indicate when and what kind of

Grade _____ Teacher _____ Dates _____

Cause / Period	Day 1					Day 2					Day 3					Day 4					Day 5				
	1	2	3	4	5	1	2	3	4	5	1	2	3	4	5	1	2	3	4	5	1	2	3	4	5
Period length too short	X		X			X	X		X		X				X	X	X		X		X			X	
Interruptions: Administrative	X	X		X	X	X	X		X	X	X	X	X		X	X	X		X	X		X			X
Student behavior	X					X	X				X		X			X			X		X		X		
Other	X							X								X							X		
Curricular expectations too high			X				X						X	X				X						X	
Teacher expectations too high		X					X					X					X							X	
Student expectations too low		X					X					X					X							X	

Figure 3.4   Inadequate Instructional Time Checksheet

inadequate instructional time problem occurred. This checksheet allows a possible collection of 125 pieces of data. The individual teacher's checksheet looks like that shown in Figure 3.4.

After five days of collecting information, the teachers gather together to tally the data. They calculate the totals for each cause and each period. They enter these individual totals into the same type of checksheet used by each teacher to collect the original data. They title this checksheet Tally of Inadequate Instructional Time—All Teachers' Gross Totals (Figure 3.5).

Studying the data reveals that most of the interruptions are administrative interruptions. The teachers decide to take this information to the school principal for discussion and possible solution. Together they decide on a goal to use only study periods and periods between classes for administrative contact of students except in emergencies. Into the *do* segment of the cycle, they decide to put the goal into action within the same pilot teachers and monitor the progress through a control

Teachers _____ , _____ , _____

_____ , _____ Dates _____

Cause	Day 1					Day 2					Day 3					Day 4					Day 5				
	1	2	3	4	5	1	2	3	4	5	1	2	3	4	5	1	2	3	4	5	1	2	3	4	5
Period length too short	5	2	0	1	3	5	2	0	3	2	5	0	0	0	1	5	1	2	3	2	5	2	1	2	1
Interruptions: Administrative	7	6	0	5	3	8	6	5	6	3	7	7	5	4	3	8	4	5	7	4	7	6	7	6	7
Student behavior	3	1	1	1	1	3	3	2	0	0	1	0	2	0	0	2	0	0	0	2	1	0	1	0	1
Other	1	0	1	0	1	0	1	0	0	1	0	0	0	0	0	0	2	1	0	1	1	0	1	0	1
Curricular expectations too high	1	0	1	0	1	0	0	1	1	1	0	0	1	1	0	0	1	1	0	0	0	0	2	1	2
Teacher expectations too high	0	0	1	0	0	0	0	1	0	0	0	0	1	1	0	0	0	1	0	0	0	0	1	0	0
Student expectations too low	1	1	1	1	1	1	2	2	1	1	1	2	2	1	2	2	2	2	1	2	2	1	2	1	2

***Figure 3.5   Tally of Inadequate Instructional Time Checksheets
All Teachers' Gross Totals***

chart. Using the data they already gathered, they develop a control chart of past experience for comparison (Figure 3.6).

Using the same five teachers, an additional five days, and similar five periods, they continue to collect data as they did before. They then enter the *study* part of the cycle by creating a new control chart on administrative interference and studying the data to see how the experiment worked. Their new control chart is shown in Figure 3.7.

After discussing the progress represented in the five-day, five-period, five-teacher pilot shown in the control chart, the teachers and school principal decide to expand the idea to the entire ninth and tenth grades. They are entering the *act* segment of the cycle. They also decide to keep track of what is happening in another sample of the tenth grade to obtain data for comparison and review. They begin the expanded solution, and thcy are into the *plan* segment again.

Figure 3.6   Control Chart of Administrative Interruptions
First Data Collection

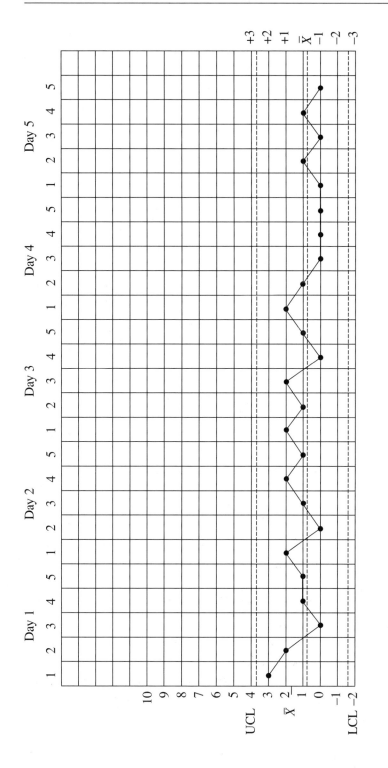

Figure 3.7 Control Chart of Administrative Interruptions
Second Data Collection

The cycle continues until not only is improvement made but perfection, as near as possible, is reached. Next, the team moves to another cause (because of assemblies and pep rallies): class period too short. The teachers begin the PDSA cycle again. The teachers' requirement of fewer interruptions in classroom instructional time begins to be met. They have used the Shewhart philosophy, the PDSA cycle, and control of the process to improve the quality of instructional time.

It's Not Easy

The tendency of many people after reading this will be to say, "That takes more time than I have. I'm too busy teaching to do administrative tasks like that." With our limited knowledge of TQM, let's ponder this. (An understanding of Deming theory will add more answers to this consideration.) TQM is everyone committed to meeting the requirements of the customer, collaboratively. The teacher is an internal customer here. "Everyone" is the principal, parents, aides, students, and other teachers. What are the roles of parents, administrators, and aides? They need to ask their internal customer, the teacher, "How can I help you?" In this example, the principal and teacher must identify how the principal can help the teacher. The parents with the teacher must identify how parents can help the teacher. The aides and the teachers must determine how the aides can help the teacher. Students too must determine their roles in helping the teacher. In this case of class period interferences, where the special cause has been identified, and if the cause is the principal's behavior, the principal must accept his or her responsibility of service to the internal customer; it is the principal's duty to find resources or negotiate a reasonable degree of service with his or her teachers. Remember that there are other people available and other options: Everyone is committed to improvement, collaboratively.

Other Tools of Quality

Shewhart's run and control charts were some of the first tools for quality improvement. Over the last 40 years additional tools have been developed. Each of these is an information gathering or information organizing tool to support the PDSA cycle of quality improvement. Listed in the following table are these tools, their purposes, and their use in the PDSA cycle.

Tool	Purpose	Cycle Use
Checklists	Record presence or absence of an observation in a process	Plan, study
Checksheets	Record measurements observed in a process	Plan, study
Graphs	Represent measurements in picture form of observations of a process	Plan, study
Brainstorming	Solicit, record, rank ideas from individuals of group	Plan, study, act
Why–why diagrams	Identify, record root causes by displaying causes by flow chart method openly on a large board or wall	Plan
Analytical troubleshooting interviews	Who, what, when, why is or is not the problem	Plan, study
Fishbone diagrams	Brainstorming recorded by grouping ideas by category along lines similar to sentence diagrams	Plan, study, act
Flow charts	Step-by-step picture of the process, sequentially listed using chart symbols	Plan, study, act
Pareto charts	Graphs showing the actual and percent of concern, 80/20 rule, law of averages	Plan, study
Run charts	Data charted to indicate trends	Plan, study, act
Histograms	Bar graphs showing how frequently something occurred	Plan, do, act
Control charts	Collect and analyze data, and predict control	Plan, study, act
Scattergrams	Used to study possible cause-and-effect relationships	Plan, study

Summary

Education processes often are under attempted control by many publics. Participants in the school learning process may interfere or intervene without objective knowledge of the processes of schooling. Their attempts can disrupt as often as they might improve learning. These efforts can create less stability, an important characteristic of an effective process.

Education problem solving will work better using Shewhart's inductive thinking. Valid data about past processes can be used to predict the future. We can control processes through knowledge of what each process is doing. Shewhart additionally contributed the PDSA cycle for problem solving. By thinking systematically and applying statistical techniques, continuing processes can be measured and improved through the use of run and control charts.

By learning the characteristics of any problem objectively from data of a valid sample, we can predict and possibly control its future. Improvement is the outcome of the reduction of special causes (causes of variation that arise because of special circumstances that are not inherent parts of the process) and common causes (causes of variation that are inherent to the system) in the learning or administrative processes of education.

Quality professionals currently use many tools of quality, including run and control charts, to identify, define, and quantify problems. Education problem solvers, intent on capturing the best information about a problem order to invent better solutions, also can use the tools of quality.

Notes

1. M. Daniel Sloan and Michael Chmel. *The Quality Revolution and Health Care*. ASQC Quality Press, Milwaukee, 1991, p. 21.

2. W. A. Shewhart. *Economic Control of Quality of Manufactured Product*. Macmillan-Van Nostrand, New York, 1931. Reissued by ASQC, Milwaukee, 1980.

3. *Ibid.*

4. *Ibid.*

Chapter 4
Deming Commitment
and Education

"Most managers are so concerned with today and with getting our own real and imagined problems settled that we are
incapable of planning corrective or positive action more than
a week ahead."

Philip Crosby

Build Quality In

Mary Walton says that Deming was 40 years old when he decided
to live with the Japanese, understand them thoroughly, and let them
understand him as a person. Then he began teaching Japanese scientists and engineers how to manufacture quality. He first taught them to
use statistics to find out what the system will do, then to design
improvements to make the system yield the best results. He taught them
that the more quality you build into anything, the less it costs. In other
words, you design quality in, not detect it in. He told them, "You can
produce quality. . . . you must carry out consumer research. . . . you
must work with vendors. . . . the consumer is the most important part
of the production line."[1] Today, at over 90 years old, Deming believes
that until the recent rebirth of quality in America, we were spending
25 percent of our resources in repair and rework.[2]

Organizations using the Deming philosophy are emulating the
Japanese success, and they are not only manufacturers. Deming wants
quality in everything we do in America—in business, industry, education, how we live, and how we teach each other and live together.
Deming sees quality as a way of life, as the moral fiber of every

American. For Deming, quality is the beginning and ending of each day. He has won many converts, among them the current president of Mexico, Carlo Salinas de Gortari, who greets his fellow business citizens first with the bywords of quality improvement, "total quality."

Deming's philosophy is embodied in his 14 points, 14 succinct guiding principles to managing quality efforts.[3] These beliefs are meant for those concerned with quality improvement, which could include school policymakers and administrators. Deming's tenets are not new. Much of his beliefs have been detailed in "humanistic," "participative," or "high-involvement management" styles. To some, his points emphasize the release of people from administrative constraints so they can find solutions to their problems. School leaders are familiar with many of Deming's considerations, but the terminology they have heard may be different. (Please note that Deming's 14 points, as listed here, have been gleaned from several sources, including works by Deming and others. The interpretations and applications of these points are those of the author.)

Constancy of Purpose

Deming's first point is to create constancy of purpose toward improvement of product and service.

For schools this means first knowing what business they are in and sticking to it. Schools are in the business of personal contribution to customers as measured by personalized service of graduates. A part of this constancy of purpose is knowing the customer and staying ahead of customer needs. Schools must think in terms of futures, always 10 to 20 years ahead of today. Schools that are constant in their purpose must change to meet customer requirements. Schools must deal with the problems of today as well as the problems of tomorrow to assure Americans that they will be in the education business of the future. As the number of private schools increases, as school vouchers and schools of choice develop, and as schools take on more and more social responsibilities, it is questionable whether or not certain schools will be in business in the future. The problems of today require attention to the quality of today's graduate as well as all the other concerns of budget, staffing, curriculum, instruction, and even public relations. To deal with tomorrow's problems, schools need to innovate in all facets, put resources into more research of what should be taught, and fund teacher and educator training. Schools also need to spread the word about constant improvement of education designs and services.

To think of the business of schools simply as "educating children" is neither long-term, specific, nor external customer driven. Being in the business of "personal contributions" of school-learned skills demands a customer focus and requires communication and development strategies to satisfy customers. Acceptance of this premise requires faith in the future and in the potential of school achievements and a sound belief in constructive parenting and teaching roles, skills, methods, materials, and equipment that will eventually match customer need. Some American schools are backing this faith and action with a customer warranty. These warranties are lifetime guarantees for qualified students who meet the regional accreditation guidelines for graduation standards. Under this warranty, a graduate who does not meet employer requirements would return to his or her school for retraining or additional training free of charge. This program is active in Colorado, Missouri, Massachusetts, Maryland, Illinois, West Virginia, and Ohio.[4] This is an indication of knowing the customer and sticking to the business.

Resource allocation for satisfying customers requires constant long-term planning, research, and retraining. This includes everyone in the school community, not just educators. Competition for the best educated work force becomes a discriminatory fact affecting students in school communities that relax in these requirements. We know that the future holds the poorest quality of lifestyle for the least educated. This concern of discrimination being an outgrowth of poor quality education must be a focus of state and federal education agencies also. It appears that these agencies aren't really sure of the focus of their business. It is obvious that they are in the political promotion business, the personal employment security business, and the extension of bureaucracy business. As rich a country as America is, it seems absurd that public education needs to beg for private funding to support public educational innovation in such critical times.

Adopt the New Management Philosophy

Deming's second point is to adopt the new philosophy. According to Deming, we are in a new economic age. Western management must be awakened to the challenge, must learn the responsibilities and take on leadership for change.

Educators and schools have no alternative to becoming institutions that support the future well-being of Americans, not suppress it or create obstacles to it. Educational institutions that exist primarily for the employment of educators for manipulation by education departments or boards of education or administrators, for the easier lifestyle of staff, or as a day-care center for parents cannot be tolerated. Educators cannot tolerate anything ineffective or wasteful or misused. American educational institutions, like American businesses, are susceptible to a just-get-by attitude, to management styles that stifle creativity, and to management behavior that is more concerned about personal security. Educational management must be committed to improvement even if management levels are eliminated. Educational management must prepare itself and others for a new world. In this new world those who come out with the first and best products and services set the rules—internationally—for everyone else. The new economy demands Americans to run the race of education knowing that those who have the most information or access to information win. There is no room for "keeping school" (maintaining the status quo) anymore at any educational level or division. The new philosophy requires leadership—doing the right things with people, not just controlling people or things.

The new philosophy of leadership relies on the abilities and skills of everyone in the school community and in the educational institution to solve problems. The new leadership represents flat organizations with open communication systems and ad hoc leadership by people who have the competence for the concern of the moment. The new philosophy perceives all minds as potential improvement resources without regard to station in the organization or status in the community. It understands that school communities must encourage dignity, self-worth, and confidence. The new philosophy needs people committed to quality improvement of education institutions and schools using all possible resources.

Build Quality in from the Beginning

Cease dependence on inspection to achieve quality. Deming's third point is to eliminate inspection on a mass basis by building quality into the product in the first place.

For educators and educational institutions, inspection on a mass basis implies that school operations that depend on mass production techniques and mass product testing should be scrutinized carefully. Educators and school communities should question the value of teaching a whole grade level of children the same thing at the same time in large classes. Educators should review the value of mass assessment of knowledge in terms of standardized test scores. People might critique the current value of the one-time instructional operation to whole groups of students who may or may not be ready for the instruction. They should review the instructional and outcome implications of standardized quality inspections through ease-of-answer computer-scored tests, which occur at set calendar periods in the school year. Does the Vermont portfolio assessment now make a little more sense? School organizations currently appear to rely, due to external pressures, almost entirely on the student-as-product test results. Test scores become the goal of all efforts. Perhaps emphasis should be placed less on test results and more on how each individual child or student is treated through curriculum and instructional individuality.

Would hospitals tell patients the following? "Our group of colon cancer surgery patients will be admitted to the hospital the day after Labor Day. Surgery and recuperation will occur during that week. Please ensure that you are registered in a wellness group of 20 patients, or we will be unable to perform the operation until next year." Are our educational institutions and schools very far from Henry Ford's assembly-line production, where the customer could have any color car he or she wanted as long as it was black?

Building quality into the product in the first place in the field of education begins at home and continues into the design of the school's instructional environment. It may take collaborative effort between legislatures, local boards of education, and school administrators to design programs for parents who send their children to public schools. Building quality in at home is a personal social responsibility of procreating persons to all other Americans. An educationally supportive home environment will need adult commitment or agencies other than schools to provide this commitment. This third-party influence on learning is sound. Children remember longer, learn more readily, and practice more intently with support from outside the school environment. We must find ways and means to provide this external environment for all levels of students.

The design of the organizational environment must be synchronized to customer service, commitment to learning and the school mission, and systematic problem solving for quality improvement. To build quality in, personal contribution must be the vision of every person in the institution or school community. Personal contribution must be "job one." Internal customer satisfaction must be everyone's goal. The instructional and curricular programs and the delivery systems must match these beliefs in allowing students as individuals to inquire, acquire, and require information within the school.

Designing quality into education requires new thinking. Currently, because students have limited time to amass information, inspection is a last-chance, futile effort to tell the student, parent, and teacher that they have succeeded or failed. Changing the design of school curricula, instructional programs, and expected outcomes requires new thinking that emphasizes improved learning processes.

Long-Term Trust

Deming's fourth point calls for an end to the practice of awarding business on the basis of price tag alone. Total costs should be minimized. Move toward a single supplier for any one item for a long-term relationship of loyalty and trust.

School administrators and managers must focus on excellence from all sources by moving toward a long-term relationship of loyalty and trust with school suppliers. The belief here applied to schools is not just one of purchasing from loyal and trustworthy single suppliers, but assuring quality in the schools by ensuring that all inputs to the school organization are tuned to the highest expectations of customers. The bitterness of substandard efforts lasts as long as the taste of just getting by. It is the board's and administration's privilege to exhort and develop the loyalty and trust of people giving their personal contribution to the schools.

This kind of leadership expects and gets only the best of effort and services. Any reason other than excellence as the benchmark for efforts or service is awarding business on the basis of price tag. Price tags are excuses for accepting anything but the highest quality kind of education service to the customer. In education, price tags are poor teacher performance evaluations, low expectations of students by universities, appointments of "good old boys" to leadership roles requiring heroes, and procrastination and delay on the part of boards in making critical decisions. Price tags are what comparison shoppers look at when they are searching for a bargain. There can be no more bargains in education. Cheat on the quality of input and you cheat on the quality of education for our children. We must minimize the total expense and the resources lost. Schools cannot afford to spend effort on anything other than helping students become the ultimate personal contributors to external customer satisfaction. It is educational management's duty to develop and maintain high standards.

The concept of a single supplier comes from the idea that few people possess enough knowledge or manpower to work effectively with more than one vendor of any item. Educators will always rely on multiple parent and multiple teaching "vendors." The trend today in business is to certify vendors, that is, describe specifications that must be met for the supplier to bid and eventually to supply. These specifications direct not only the work standards but also the process controls, the quality assurance standards, and continuous site visits to ensure compliance. Businesses will not buy from uncertified vendors. This idea might contain some merit for educators. The state of Tennessee, in its original Career Ladder Program for educators, required a portfolio of specifications, quality assurances, work standards, and process control in addition to several site visits from evaluators who were unfamiliar with the evaluated teacher. Consider too the parent as "vendor" of a precious resource, the child. In the internal customer concept, the parent is serving the teacher. Teachers could identify reasonable specifications for parents relative to the home learning environment and certify parents who will cooperate. Guardians and agencies would be included in the assurance of a well-prepared student to inquire, acquire, and require.

In all this interpretation, schools are not free. They require responsible commitment from everyone. Citizens would no more be allowed to put obstacles in the way of public educators than to interfere with public medical, police, or fire protection personnel who are doing their duty. Parents, guardians, and agencies must realize that education cannot do it all. Educators cannot be parents, nurses, therapists, sociologists, dieticians, psychiatrists, leisure time directors, gang mediators, community emergency coordinators, or siblings to students. They may be available for appropriate agencies to provide services to children, but under strict limitations (such as after school). Schools have limited resources. Like businesses, they will fail if they do not stick to their business.

One of the problems of American education may be that human service agencies outside the school perceive the school as a good bet to get agency business done at lower costs with a ready-made set of helping hands. These agencies should perceive that they are part of a school community that falls within the realm of responsible commitment to school external customership. Agencies relying on schools to do their work are placing a business burden and an additional cost of quality on the schools. Outside agents of any kind which desire to use the schools for their own purpose sap the resources and efforts of educators from their primary mission, satisfying the external identified customer. This is simply an additional cost to the quality of a graduate.

Continual Improvement

Point five is to improve constantly and forever the system of production and service, to improve the quality and productivity and thus constantly decrease costs.

The Japanese have a word for it, *kaizen,* which when understood "integrates respect for and awareness of the forces of processes."[5] It means "continuous, incremental quality improvements."[6] To the Japanese kaizen means knowing in your heart that quality pays; it pays in employment security, expanded respect, increased personal contributions, delighted customers, and a long-term positive reputation. Kaizen simply means improvement, ongoing improvement involving everyone in the schools. Kaizen assumes that "our way of life, including marriage, family, social, home, and spiritual or work life deserves constant attention for improvement."[7]

Deming and his colleague Juran raised the concept of kaizen to new levels in Japan in the 1950s and 1960s using Shewhart's statistical tools. Since then kaizen includes a focus to improve the design and development of the process as much as leaning toward constructive improvement of the historical process. Kaizen requires committed management to be implemented. It must be perceived by others in planning, communicating, involving, and facilitating constructive improvement of school programs. It must be observed by all, not secreted in the boardrooms.

In schools and educational institutions kaizen begins at the top. Once the board of education, administration, and support services are committed, they begin to "walk the talk." These management attitudes will flow throughout the organization. "Words themselves have no power; it is the spirit of the words given by the speaker" that communicates commitment to the entire school community.[8] Talking kaizen improvement, without the spirit of intent and the associated action, is communicated faster than rumors.

When education management begins to ask "How can we do better?" ("we" meaning management, not others), education will improve. Putting out fires is not improving processes. Creating model programs will not improve schools. Higher education idealizing without thorough knowledge of the schools is not improvement. It will take something like Shewhart's problem-solving approach and the matching of models or ideals to improve education in America.

Everyone associated with education—federal, state, and local agencies, and higher education institutions—needs to accept kaizen and apply the tools of quality.

Train Everyone

Point six is to institute training on the job.

Shewhart's thoughts and applications and Deming's 14 points and their applications must be learned by everyone in the educational community. In addition, everyone needs continuous technical training specific to their role as boardmember, parent, teacher, administrator, division chief, or aide. Everyone needs to learn nonstatistical and statistical problem solving, decision making, customership, and customer-focus strategies and the seven principles of TQE. This training must be different from previous training. Not only must it include everyone, but it must be done at as little sacrifice to the learner as possible.

Everyone a Leader

Point seven is to institute leadership. The aim of management should be to help people and machines and gadgets do a better job. Management needs an overhaul.

Educational leaders must begin to remove obstacles in the paths of progress of others. These leaders should look at policies, regulations, and guidelines as possible obstacles to progress; these leaders must realize that each time they create direction, policy, legislation, or regulation they are actually limiting others. Educational leaders must support excellence in customership between people; they must trust that if they have done their job as leaders, people can determine their own requirements.

There is a difference between management and leadership. Management relates to things and equipment and the people controlling them. Leadership relates directly to the soul of people and their owned actions. Leaders influence people positively in the right direction toward the vision. Leaders focus on facilitating the people closest to the problem in their own process improvement. Effective leaders encourage involvement, ownership, and accountability of problem solving and decisions by others. Good leaders also support and celebrate successes with those accountable.

Leadership in TQM is shared, shared among those who are the most competent and committed to the problem at the time. Leaders may come from team memberships rather than appointments. As groups gather to focus on problems, teams can be formed within structured focuses. Parents can be leaders of curricular problems with teachers mixed in teams. Students can be leaders of learning problems mixed in teams with parent and teachers. Board members can collaborate with teachers and community members in team actions; leadership may eventually come from an individual who is knowledgeable and competent in the subject rather than an elected or appointed leader. External customers can form teams to determine needs. In true TQ, no one waits around for an authorized nod to solve a customer problem; the person who sees the problem and has the knowledge and competence to lead becomes the leader. The education of our children can't wait.

Leadership in education may come from other than appointed or authorized means. Authenticity of concern, the existence of a problem, and the will to resolve it with others may be the criteria for those who shall lead and those who share leadership. Leadership in education can no longer wait for those with status, those in charge, or those who get paid to do it. If there is any waiting or procrastination in quality improvement, it's obvious that the appointed leader is either too busy or is lost in his or her priorities. America can't wait any longer; we all must lead, follow, or get out of the way. But we can't just stand there.

Fearless People

Deming's point eight is to drive out fear so that everyone may work effectively.

People cannot put on their best performance unless they feel secure and unafraid to express their ideas, take risks, ask questions, and seek new information or solutions. Deming saw fear in American industry, something he did not see in his early days in Japan. In America he saw people driven by job security, resulting in fear of not pleasing superiors, and fear of loss of pay for performance, restricting quality achievements. These types of fears hold people back from doing their jobs better.

Psychologists tell us that fear causes resistance to change, inhibits open communications, and closes the mind to new knowledge. Much of the "restrictive self" in each of us today closes our minds to new opportunities. This restrictive behavior resulted from schooling, military, and church practices designed to keep us safe, to help us conform, and to ensure achievement within the norms. It has helped us homogenize society, but it has also restricted improvement. That same "do it this way or else" motivation holds back many teachers and students in our schools from exploring new worlds.[9] This same motivation keeps the federal and state departments of education from seeing their real business and customer focus in relation to local educational agencies. This same motivation restricts all of America from perceiving and sensitively reacting to the education emergency blowing up in our faces. This unseen authority of the old self hovers over all of us and our progress; it casts shadows of restriction rather than the light of construction in educational growth.

Our future depends on support of individual constructive efforts, on willingness to recognize innovation and support it, on individual and team goal setting to invent futures, and on new job designs for parents, teachers, and students. Anything that prohibits free, open, and honest communication should be investigated. A quality school organization exhibits a special courage and spirit, a willingness to improve without fear.

Working Together

Point nine is to break down barriers between departments. People must work as a team to foresee problems of production and use that may be encountered with the product or service.

Whatever it is that separates educational groups from joint efforts must be challenged. In educational communities, it is important to be linked as an internal customer team serving the external consuming organization or customer. Egos need to be refashioned into a bonded collaboration between parents, teachers, students, administrators, and all others.

Imagine teams of students responsible for supporting each other for research, independent study, and academic and management concerns. (In Japan they call them *hahns*.) Imagine teams of parents sharing ways to better bring up their children. Imagine matrix teams of people sharing better ways to serve external customers. Imagine multiple teams, setting goals, solving problems, and making decisions, believing that what they are doing is satisfying—and the right thing to do. Imagine the increased motivation to serve each other because everyone is owner of the problem, the solution, the progress of the solution, and the final achievement. What a cause for celebration, when everyone feels a share of the accomplishment.

Teaming is not just grouping people together. Teams are goal-oriented and use multipowered thinking. Teams reduce dissonance in decision implementation through consensus. Teams identify their own focus and efforts and problems and solutions. The team approach might begin with a quality improvement team at a department or grade level with a variety of members. It might first do a quality audit of current perceptions of practices in the organization using the Baldrige Award categories.[10] The Baldrige Award categories provide a path for educators to follow in school improvement. These categories are titled "Leadership in the Quality Effort," "Information Collection and Analysis," "Strategic Planning for Quality," "Human Resource Use for Quality," "Quality Assurance," "Quality Results," and "Customer Satisfaction." Each category embraces standards which can be used like regional accreditation standards.

Educators can gain baseline data about their school or community organization by developing a survey instrument based on the categories and standards and surveying a sample population of the organization. These survey results will offer data for development of the goals and objectives of a total quality education plan and also help in prioritizing continual improvement efforts.

Do It by Ourselves

Deming's tenth point is to eliminate all slogans, exhortations, and targets for the work force which ask for zero defects and new levels of performance.

Educational leaders are not usually slogan broadcasters, although cheerleading is a common educational practice. There has been some quota bargaining in the sense of school racial integration brought on by Congress and the justice system and some quota targeting to assist student dropouts and college entrance requirements. There have been new efforts in gaining increases in performance as judged by standardized tests. Deming's emphasis is to allow individuals or teams of people to set their own quotas, slogans, and targets of performance. Experience has shown that when educators or teams set their own goals and targets, they usually exceed those of management.

Research has shown that possibly more than 80 percent of the problems of achieving quality are the result of processes within the system.[11] Perhaps 20 percent are problems outside the system. In education, this means that success is more a design, system, or management problem than an instructional problem. This conclusion points the finger of responsibility directly at legislatures, monitoring agencies, school boards, and administrators that control the policies that promote 80 percent of the problem.

Legislative, bureaucratic, and board policies are often counterproductive to individualized instruction, innovation, or providing flexible learning opportunities or environments according to the mental or physical developmental needs of learners. Consider the secondary school traditional daily, weekly, and monthly school period length and number, the basis of the accreditation guidelines for graduation credit. Consider the psychological limitations placed on learners by a 55- or 70-minute or other period length of course study, five or six times a day. Is it a constructive human learning process to compartmentalize learning operations like a series of machine operations, hour in hour out, day in day out, week in week out, month in month out, year in year out? Yet most of our schools reflect this policy and regulation. Consider also the student and teacher policy manuals developed to regulate behaviors in schools. Compare them to the Nordstrom Employee Handbook. Although Nordstrom currently is being challenged in the application of its guiding principle, it is succeeding where other stores are failing. The two-sided card says, "Welcome to Nordstrom. We're glad to have you with our company. Our number one goal is to provide outstanding customer service. Set both your personal and professional goals high. We have great confidence in your ability to achieve them. Rule number one is to use your own good judgment in all situations. There will be no additional rules. Please feel free to ask your department managers and store managers any question, any time."[12] Educational policy is elaborate and restrictive. It attempts to set goals for many students and professionals who are entirely capable of setting their own goals.

Deming says that people should be allowed to set their own goals and targets. People can enrich their lives, jobs, and responsibilities by identifying what they believe is their potential. People can capture accountability through their own desire, not administration's imposition. Students should set learning goals for themselves. The goals of education should be driven from the bottom up. People nearest to the problem should share in all the information about the problem, and they should devise resolutions for the problem. Administrative commitment shows when management supports success by helping in the administrative side of measuring, tracking, and displaying progress, really making improvement easier and really serving others. Imagine what it would mean for a student body and teaching staff to see administration in this service role. Imagine what it would mean for parents. Managing others is the old way of thinking; helping people manage themselves is today's need.

Staying Within the Lines

Point eleven is to eliminate numerical quotas for the work force. Eliminate numerical quotas for management. Eliminate the worker and management styles reinforced by management numerical quotas.

At first one might say, "Well, this doesn't fit education or schools. We have no quotas. He's talking about manufacturers who say to their work force, '50,000 units this month' or '20 home sales a month' or 'a

car a minute' or 'increase by six per day.'" Business does this to stimulate others to make a profit for the company and to provide incentives.
Quotas in business stimulate achievement. Schools, however, are run
by quotas without incentives.

Ever hear these familiar words? "We must cover two chapters per
week." "Your reading assignment will cover the first 30 pages of the
novel." "We can only teach to the contracted pupil-teacher ratio of 25
to 1." Do any educators think in the following terms? "This semester
has 90 days, so let's see what I'll be able to teach." Or "I'm allocated
45 teachers, a 5-period day, with 1125 students, so that means we can
teach 225 periods of 25 students per class." Almost without thinking
about it, educators struggle with numerical quotas and administration
by numbers. It is now nearly the nature of education to be ruled by
numbers. If schools are essentially a numbers game, then who really is
the customer? Is it the comptroller of the budget, the fiscal authority,
the accreditation agency, the assistant principal in charge of scheduling, the state policymakers determining the length of the school year,
the federal government determining the number of students per
teacher, the chief negotiators of the teacher master agreement—or the
consuming external customer of the graduate?

The intent of administration by number is admirable, if the intent
is to use time efficiently, keep costs down, provide order to the institution, and provide some equity to teachers or students. But what is the
actual impact of a calculator running the schools? What is the actual
impact on the level of learning and teaching by these "numerical
styles"? Number crunching in education cannot become the ultimate
bottom line. If numbers are the bottom line, then people, learning, and
customers are not, at least in the schools they are not. In schools, numbers are just the white lines of the road. They are not the destination.
When the situation fits, they suggest the lane to drive in. The individual driver eventually determines which lane to use, when to cross the
lines, and when to pull to the shoulder. White lines have little valuable
depth. People do.

People Have Unlimited Potential

Point twelve is to remove barriers that rob people of pride of workmanship. Eliminate the annual rating system or merit system.

In his interviews with American workers, Deming found them voicing complaints about management support, inadequate or worn equipment, supplies defective and short, and treatment of people by managers as if they were expendable. He, like many business consultants, had found work forces that believed there was a disregard for workers on the part of management. Quality consultants have found that management often is willing to pay people for making poorer product in favor of production quotas. The talk in businesses like this, untouched by TQM, is still the same today. Manufacturers that insist on profit over people reap the work life problems found in worker interviews.

The talk in many teacher lounges isn't that different these days. "They're cutting the music and art next; there goes our curriculum again." "Thank goodness we have a teacher contract so at least we'll know what to expect." "There isn't enough money to keep the audio-visual equipment running; we'll just have to schedule it better." "The computer is down again, fourth time this month." "Those electrical outlets never worked; I've always just brought an extension cord from home." "Yes, it's time for school pictures again. Without the profit from the pictures we wouldn't have some teaching supplies." "Why sure, whether you're a good or a bad teacher, the pay is the same." "Yes, he graduated last year, but I'm not proud of what he learned."

The barriers that rob people of rightful pride in their work in business are the same in education. Quality of work life issues are generally based on communication, resource allocation, resource development, belief in people as the best resource, and customers. These issues are administrative inadequacies; they are the barriers to success. Performance ratings are additional, psychological barriers.

Deming's view of performance rating is unique. According to Deming, it is not a question of how much a student has learned, but what he or she will do with it that should be graded. "I give all my students As, for I really cannot tell what they will do with what they have learned." He believes that he has pressed his students to their full potential of knowledge acquisition; now how well will they perform? He doesn't know. Deming trusts that the student will do the best he or she is able, according to personal goals the student has set, within the system in which he or she works.

Use of administrative performance standards may be more of a de-motivator than a motivator. External standards developed and applied from outside the individual are known as stimuli. Properly chosen and developed, these stimuli might encourage appropriate behaviors. Individuals may perform to a greater potential when they establish their own guidelines. When allowed to set their own performance standards, people usually exceed any that might have been set for them.

Teachers and principals have tried to move away from the use of grading. Teachers generally seem less positive about administrator ratings than boards or administration. In both cases, students and teachers often perceive the value of evaluation as the means of getting an A. Evaluations are opportunities for recognition or reward. People may wish that A ratings are reflections of excellence and recognition for excellence, but we must recognize the subjectivity of the evaluation process. And that is what Deming is talking about. Grading, or rating, promotes the pursuit of recognition rather than the pursuit of excellence.

Grading and rating are processes that reflect the limitations or behaviors set by persons other than the student or educator. If this is so, success, progress, and improvement are all defined within the narrow limits of a superordinate. People might only do well enough to get the grade expected. They "satisfice." They are robbed of pride of ownership of their success and ownership of their acquisition of knowledge in favor of recognition for achieving someone else's standards.

People expand their mental and physical efforts for their own reasons—a sense of achievement, self-fulfillment, personal growth, advancement within the system, recognition from others. The TQE environment needs to be designed around personally set goals, personal achievement, personal self-fulfillment, personal growth, and personal promotion with recognition occurring more naturally after success rather than within a periodic grading or rating calendar. Why not get out of the business of rating altogether, and just celebrate successes as they happen? Why not measure processes, not people?

Everyone a Learner

Institute a vigorous program of education and self-improvement for everyone is Deming's thirteenth point.

Study, learn, improve yourself. Sharpen your mind because as part of the whole organization you will affect the thoughts and progress of others and the whole organization. There is the story of the hospital custodian with whom the brain surgeon was spending valuable time during his busy surgery schedule. When asked why the surgeon could spend time with him when the surgeon's skills were so needed and expensive, the custodian simply replied, "Me and the doctor, we save lives." [14] Modern educational improvement means everyone contributes. These new contributions are not just physical, but they are mental, informational, problem-solving ideas that should come from everyone. The new role of the educational leader will be collector of everyone's thinking. Without new thoughts, the education organization will become stagnant.

Everyone in the schools is in the same business: personal contribution to the customer. It isn't just the student or the teacher who is responsible for quality improvement and customer satisfaction. Everyone must learn new information, expand his or her self-confidence and risk-taking ability. Each of us must know and understand that an educational enterprise is where people take risks, try new things, and have minds open to new knowledge of all kinds. Educational institutions made of people who refuse to learn and grow will hold back the whole organization. A constructive learning environment is a fragile ecosystem dependent on positive, progressive behaviors on the part of everyone. It is woefully dependent on love, positive regard for self and others, and individual caregiving. One selfish, careless person can crash the whole organization. What happens to a football team in the moment of battle when just one player decides to run his own play?

The lifeblood of education and of educational quality improvement is personal development and lifelong learning habits for everyone. That's the name of the game. If people cannot exemplify the reason schools exist in their own lives, then they should go to an organization where learning is not important, if they can find one. It will take study and investigation to understand each one of these 14 points. There is no shortage of knowledge. There is no shortage of good people, just a shortage of people who want and know how to do better. The information exists to do better. People just don't know it. Isn't that a condemnation of American education in itself?

Education at War

Point fourteen is to put everyone to work on the transformation. The transformation is everybody's responsibility.

Educational management at the federal, state, and local levels must initiate the institution of these 14 points and the application of them through the continual use of the PDSA cycle. First, identify a problem, form a team, narrow the problem to a clear definition, investigate and study the process, collect quantifiable information, analyze it, and measure some more. Second, form a goal and then a plan to resolve the problem, carry it out on a small scale, observe it, measure it, and record the results. Third, study the results; determine what needs to be revised or if it can be instituted. Fourth, implement the solution on a larger scale, use what you learned from the pilot, look for side effects, and continue the cycle. Remember that all of this is in light of the internal and external customership principles.

Remember our nation during the Persian Gulf War. Over a period of months a fragmented nation unified to over 80 percent in support of the president to free Kuwait. Because of the transformation of American sentiment from confusion to concurrence, the war was decisive, short, and successful. Many elements played a part in the victory, but none was accidental. People realized that they were an important part of a significant plan. They knew the goal and they owned some part of it with blood, sweat, or mind. Americans unified for something more significant than themselves. They unified because they were proud and believed in certain principles and abilities. They believed in a certain quality of life.

Americans now need to revive this same spirit in a war against a lower quality of life, a physical and mental bondage caused by joblessness and poverty due to an inability to play in an educated international competition. We have no choice but to work for a transformation of American education.

Summary

Deming's 14 points are a statement of the belief that within any organization, its people are its most important resource. And like any resource, it can be of no value unless it is used to its potential. People are not machines; they own the capacity to think beyond an operation, a process, or a policy. They can use this potential for the improvement of almost anything they can measure and some things they can't.

The foundation for tapping this potential lies within the following beliefs:

1. Knowing your business, how and what satisfies customers, and sticking to that business.

2. Realizing that the world is changing and we must change our leadership style to tap into everyone's potential.

3. Designing quality into home and educational environments, ensuring a fitting condition for excellence in the beginning.

4. Maintaining high expectations in loyalty and trust of all inputs to the schooling process; expecting and demanding the best of parents and others.

5. Constantly improving everything we do, personally, in our families, socially, and at work. Kaizen must begin at the top or it won't happen.

6. Training in TQ for everyone in the school community.

7. Sharing leadership based on knowledge and competence first, and authority second.

8. Taking risks without fear and making constructive efforts to improve education.

9. Breaking down whatever barriers exist between people that prevent school quality improvement.

10. Allowing people to determine their own goals, targets, and quotas, and giving people the latitude to use their own judgment.

11. Eliminating administration, teaching, or learning by numbers.

12. Eliminating artificial reasons for mandates, fostering instead ownership and involvement for accountability.

13. Seeking, gaining, and using new information continually.

14. Attacking concerns of poor quality education. Everyone in the educational community must work together.

Notes

1. Mary Walton. *The Deming Management Method.* Perigree Books, Putnam, New York, 1986, pp. 13–14.

2. Lloyd Dobyn. "Ed Deming Wants Big Changes, and He Wants them Fast." *Smithsonian* (August 1990): 74–82.

3. W. Edwards Deming. *Out of the Crisis.* Massachusetts Institute of Technology, Cambridge, 1986, pp. 23–24.

4. Massachusetts School Boards Association. "Trends, Guaranteed Graduates." *School Board News* (January 1991): 1.

5. K. Imai. *Kaizen.* McGraw-Hill, New York, 1986, pp. 3–5.

6. *Ibid.*

7. *Ibid.*

8. Lou Tice. "Investments in Excellence." Videotape. The Pacific Institute, Seattle, 1986.

9. *Ibid.*

10. U.S. Department of Commerce. "Baldrige Award Application." Washington, D.C., 1990.

11. H. S. Haller. "Statistical Business Management." Statistical Studies Inc. presentation, Bay Village, Ohio, 1987.

12. Nordstrom Inc. "Nordstrom Employee Handbook." Seattle, Wash., 1988.

Chapter 5
Principles of
Total Quality Education

"The new frontiers of human creativity in every area lie in information systems and their utilization."

J. J. Servan Scriber

Using the Information

Every educator has believed at one time or another, "I know that there are answers to these problems; I just don't see them." The purpose of this chapter is to synthesize the elements of TQM and offer some guiding principles for TQE based on Shewhart and Deming. Educators may, with this particular chapter, begin to see that the elements of TQ are similar for all organizations. TQM has been used by many enterprises worldwide, and there is a relationship between school improvement and business improvement. Most organizations using TQ have developed definitions and principles similar to these. The Britannica Educational Corporation has summarized TQ in this manner.

What is quality?
A quality product or service is one that meets or exceeds customer expectations.

What is total quality?
A commitment to excellence in which all functions of an organization focus on continual improvement, resulting in increased customer satisfaction.

Total quality is:

A management philosophy and operating methodology.

Breakthrough thinking, thinking differently.

A structured, disciplined approach to identifying and solving problems, and institutionalizing the improvement gained.

Conveyed actions by management.

Top down.

Long-term.

Supported by quality tools.

A permanent solution, a way of life.

Quality is not:

A new program.

The same old way of thinking.

Fire fighting.

Conveyed by slogans.

Bottom up.

Short-term.

Driven by quality tools.

A quick fix.

Your customers expect perfection:

We all have customers; they may be both internal and external.

Total quality fundamental questions:

1. Who are my customers?
2. What do they need?
3. What are their measurements, their expectations?
4. What is my product or service?
5. Does my product or service meet or exceed their expectations?
6. What is the process for improving my product or service?

7. What corrective action is needed to improve my processes?

Total quality improvement steps:
Document the process actions.
Establish key customer based measures.

Characterize:
Collect data on key customer based measures.
Analyze data to identify root causes or problem areas.
Simplify.
Eliminate all redundancies, rework, and waste.
Standardize the process.

Automate:
Where feasible and appropriate, automate process steps.

Key links between quality, productivity, and customer satisfaction:
True improvement in services lowers costs, lowers prices, and increases customer satisfaction.

Key factors for TQ success:
Management leadership, top down, committed, and active.
Clearly understood and agreed on goals.
Breakthrough thinking, not the same old way.
Appropriate process performance measures.
Teamwork.
Training.
Sharing, promoting, and reinforcing success.

Process improvement tools:
Flow charts.
Cause-and-effect diagrams.
Histograms.

Pareto charts.

Scattergrams.

Run charts.

Control charts.

Checksheets.[1]

These are the elements of TQ. Certainly much of this is being done in some educational communities already under other forms and other titles. But it might be valuable for educators to speak the same terms as others in the business community. That is what it is all about—helping people speak the same national language whether they are in business or in education.

A Declaration of TQE

Based on what has been discussed so far, we can create principles of TQE. These principles are of what is expected of people in TQE enterprises. They are similar to many business TQM principles: they are the foundation for a TQ school. Let's call these principles the Declaration of TQE.

1. Total management commitment—to make management's role in TQE clear to everyone, so there is no confusion or conjecture about the change toward quality. Cohesive followership relies on board of education, administrator, and parent commitment to this first step.

2. Customer-first focus, always—to ensure that internal customers are serviced to their requirements so that external customers receive satisfactory service. The customer first philosophy demands an open communication loop from the school to the customer and back, which reflects an adjusted curriculum and instruction to meet changing customer requirements.

3. Commitment to teamwork—a team is led by members and composed of anyone in the school community who has a concern. It uses nonstatistical and statistical problem-solving approaches. It is committed to team goal setting, measurement and display, and achievement. Teams use the PDSA cycle.

4. Commitment to self-management and leadership—learning is something only the learner can be accountable for, but it can be

aided by others. Effective learning is solitary. Clearing obstacles to learning requires help from others in the form of leadership.

5. Commitment to continuous improvement—requires the kaizen attitude of improving all of life, open information and communication systems, an environment that induces growth through continuous training, and learning for everyone.

6. Commitment to belief in individual and team potential—reflected in all processes, services, and requirements. Everyone is an enabler of others, and this is reflected in his or her own behavior and personal contribution to the quality effort. High expectations are the norm because people reach them all the time.

7. Commitment to quality—a major role of our life is to serve others by knowing and meeting their requirements. A commitment to quality means helping others. Negotiation, conflict resolution, communication, and information sharing are expected practices.

Management Commitment

Much of the purpose of any educational plan is to get everyone going in the same direction. Schools moving toward any vision need someone to lead, to define the direction, and to paint the picture. The role of management is to assemble clearly a unity of purpose for everyone to follow. To assure this unity everyone must be trained in the Declaration of TQE, beginning with board members, administrators, and parents. A public acceptance of the declaration in front of students and teachers will impress everyone with the seriousness of quality improvement.

Management commitment can also be shown by the appointment of a quality improvement council made up of the board chairman, superintendent, senior union leaders, parents, and other administrators. This council's first tasks are to develop a tentative plan for TQ pilot programs and a training plan. As people receive training, they will give input to revise the tentative plan accordingly. Part of this TQE plan will focus on quality improvement, develop and oversee education quality improvement forces, and evaluate and recognize their efforts.

This council's progress would be the first item on every board of education agenda, and it would report at length on all the quality efforts in the schools. The council itself should meet weekly until the quality effort becomes owned by others. It should have its own budget allocation and line item of the budget as well as authority to influence other line items. It should request resources for persons and processes for quality improvement.

The major focus of this council the first year should be awareness of TQE concepts and development of ownership of the Declaration of TQE. Opportunities must be given for everyone to buy in to the mission of personal contribution to external and internal customers. The council should be a mentor monitor that ensures success of the quality improvement process. The council should focus on projects initiated at the lowest levels with training available as needed by the teams. It should ensure the success of teams by monitoring the type of goals, efforts, and resources needed and giving administration support. It is the council's responsibility to ensure recognition for success.

Management Commitment and Politics

Public education enterprises by their current status are political entities, subject to all the problems of power and influence. These systems are tremendously affected by continual efforts at building coalitions within and without the system, as well as through the democratic process. Politics in either sense is inescapable. Both political processes are good in light of the principles of democracy currently in vogue. But when these processes are corrupted by special interest, self-interest, employment security, maintenance of the status quo, then these political processes become obstacles to TQE. As political processes, they should be subject to process control and continual improvement and to the principles of the Declaration of TQE.

Subverting the political process to one's self-interest, although ethically acceptable in the nineties in Congress, is truly not for the common good in education. Self-interest is not internal or external customership—at best it might be internal service to one another. This is a business burden, a cost of quality education problem. The resources, the effort, the discipline, the focus, the vision, the time, and the finances used to fuel this self-interest are expenses that do not contribute to educational service to the external customer. None of these expenses is accountable as personal contributions. These are costs spent for the satisfaction of individuals using the education system for selfish gain. These politicians are stealing from the public; even worse, they are cheating children of their right to a quality education. Spending precious resources on doing things wrong or doing the wrong things are expenses that result in poorer quality education. We must realize that there is little or no true value added to the product through these efforts. This business burden cost to quality is not affordable in an environment with limited resources, such as our schools. Only the very wealthy can afford this kind of luxury.

Cost-effectiveness in the political process can be ensured at least two ways. First, there must be an external educational focus on the customer in any political effort. Coalitions, selections, and elections must be based on participants who at the least verbalize and have proven their commitment to external customer satisfaction in education. Second, coalition building and selection and election processes must be submitted to the PDSA cycle to ensure that customer concern exists. The need for the coalitions should be based on publicized statistical information and problem solving. This use of the PDSA cycle would keep efforts in front of the public and place the political process within controls. No coalition within the school could be built, no applicant enjoined, and no candidate elected without the necessary proof that can predict continual improvement. Imagine political efforts where obvious progress is clearly shown through statistical evidence rather than popularity. Every political participant could use the PDSA cycle for his or her favorite projects in pilots within the system long before a coalition was needed and long before appointment or election. Any politician could seek office through competent use of the PDSA cycle and prove his or her competence in continual improvement and commitment to the Declaration of TQE.

Wherever there are people, there is the attraction to power and influence. The point of this discussion is to find a means wherein Americans can continue to maintain our democracy and focus efforts on quality improvement. Much of traditional schooling in the public sector has been characterized by not being able to stick to the business. In the competitive arena outside the school, businesses that lack working information systems internally and externally and that do not maintain contact and focus on the customer fail. When businesses get into enterprises they know nothing about, they fail.[2] What is the business of a quality educational enterprise? It is the personal contribution of the service agent graduate to that external customer as measured by personalized service. Efforts, decisions, strategies, and plans that do not focus on these aspects of the education business should be allowed little or no attention.

Customer First

Few educators or educational administrators understand the businesses, industries, or most of the organizations to which they are sending their 13-year processed graduate. Educators too often lack an understanding and clear response to their external customer. The recent attempts in adopt-a-school programs indicate this clearly. Educators wanted help from business, but not their collaboration. So businesses were relegated to roles of supplying materials that were not in the school budget and asked to help celebrate school events. Few programs have advanced far enough to negotiate the expectations of both schools and business to an improvement in the quality of education. Seldom have these adopting businesses attempted to identify the requirements for graduating students. In other forums, business has asked that graduates possess minimal skills in problem solving, command of the English language, self-discipline, and the ability to acquire and apply new knowledge.[3] These requirements seem rather low relative to the annual expense of elementary and secondary schooling that costs Americans more than $135 billion a year.[4] These kinds of frustrated determinations of school expectations coupled with the $10 billion or so that private enterprise spends annually on training will overprice our products and services in the world market. Other nations will produce educated work forces more cheaply. Other international companies will price themselves below us for similar goods and services because they do not carry this educational burden of cost.

Education serves three functions: to promote American culture, to prepare individuals for participation in the political system, and to prepare individuals for the economic system. As such, all three are one: preparing individuals for an economic future in an American culture. Business must do a better job of identifying its requirements. It cannot do this until business moves out of its short-term crisis planning and management styles and moves into world class customer focus. There is a tendency to use smokestack management (industrial versus information age management) based on the thinking that man is just another machine. Businesses must move into the state of the future just as education must. Both must determine the quality of business they are now in and the quality of the business in which they will succeed in the future. They both must fix their focus on the following questions. "Who are and will be our customers 20 years from now?" "What will be the demands, needs, expectations, and wants?" "How are we responding and how will we respond to these requirements?" Business knows that short-term planning is only good for one play; it doesn't fit the whole game. We as a nation cannot build successful world leadership in business or education by playing catch-up as we currently are with other industrialized and third world countries. We must take charge of our businesses and our training to be business leaders.

Kindergarten through twelfth-grade education takes at least 12 to 13 years to produce its product. The customer whom business serves today will be different 13 years from now. Schools, if they are to meet the world challenge, must know what business will require in the years 2001, 2005, 2010. More than ever we need an American business-education consensus. The definition of quality is really no different to Cadillac, IBM, Stew Leonard's, or Greenbriar Elementary School. The schools are, in part, suppliers to the American economy and rely on business to define customer expectations. It may be necessary for local boards of education to reach out and demand business to identify its requirements. Until then, schools have good reasons not to perform and to comply with their shareholders' desires. Education certainly has little ability to satisfy its customer until it knows the requirements.

Customer First, Internally

Internal customership is second only to external customership. Internal customers must articulate and clarify what each expects of the other. In order to do this, each person in the education community might first list four to six of the most important people in the education environment with whom each spends 75 to 80 percent of his or her time. Then list the specific products or services each provides these customers; then sit down with each customer and review these together. Ask what it is that really delights them when the service is performed well. Ask what is needed from them to perform the service well. Write these things down under five sections:

- Name, Responsibility of Customer
- Their Expected Services/Products
- Criteria to Delight Them
- Need from Them
- What's in it for Me, the Server

Together review this with administration, suggesting what is needed from it to accomplish the services. Discuss it thoroughly so there is no ambivalence in the expectations. Sign it and date it. Call it an affirmation of service and keep it displayed where you can see and review it easily. Parents could do this with teachers; eighth-grade teachers could do it with ninth-grade teachers; college students could do it with professors; local education agencies could do it with state agencies; state agencies could do it with federal agencies. If the expectations are reasonable, then it is only appropriate that resources be allocated or developed to satisfy customers. If there are no resources, expect no service. Resources include training provided for people to serve internal customers. Additional equipment may be needed, and additional personnel may be required. Internal customer communication and the development of requirements quantify educational positions, clarify the importance of resources, and strengthen the process of serving each other as internal customers.

Customer First Culture

Enough research has been done to show that people under normal circumstances will do everything they can to meet the expectations others have of them. These affirmations of service are not role descriptions but internal customer agreements that are personally customized and reviewed annually with each internal customer. Revision will occur where the school must adjust to changing requirements of external customers. Behind this design is the basic premise that Americans must learn customer service, and in the end, customer service is people delighting others by serving them. Grady Regas of Chili's and Grady's Good Times restaurants says, "It's blowin' them away . . . doing more for people than they would expect."[5] In the customer service view, everyone in education will at some time or another be in contact with a customer in need; it is this moment of truth that makes the difference. People judge a restaurant, a manufacturer, a school, a college, a department, or a division often by the caliber of contact received from those serving them. The contact is major no matter how minor the service or the server. Each contact is measured by the customer's own expectations or requirements. Customership requires people treating each other with respect, courtesy, and care— an obvious desire to understand another's needs and a willingness to do the best to provide the service. Imagine the change when people welcome customer requests. Stew Leonard's stores are enjoyable because they practice the principle, "the customer is always right," and stories of Nordstrom's customer service are legendary. Chili's and Grady's restaurants are attractive to customers because of service. Imagine if service requests in the education sector were received with a smile and the statement, "It's my pleasure to help you." Imagine the impact on students. Customer service becomes everybody's job. Isn't that a personal contribution?

A focus on the customer first always needs to become the way things are done in education. It must become the measure of career and personal success. Education leaders must treat people as customers, verbalizing and displaying behaviors of the customer service ethic. This ethic displayed by school leaders will encourage the same behaviors from others. Pride in the school and ownership of its product will grow from personal customer service. People will realize that "me, the housekeeper, and the doctor, we save lives."[6]

Commitment to Teamwork

Why a commitment to teaming rather than political coalitions of just plain groups? The answer comes from the distinctive character of teams and the research on effective teams. Educators may say that in their school, in their central office, in their college, and in their department people work well together and these groups can be characterized as teams. Some educators would advance, too, that their school has multiple committees that are composed of a variety of members from multiple populations, a representation of the totality of the school participants. Current renewed emphasis on site-based management councils is a good example of this. These might also be called teams from one point of view, if they actually focus on customers and quality improvement. It could be more likely that these groups have been designed more for representative input, extra hands for the short term, or ownership expansion of a problem that upper management lacks the will to solve. Teams are not administratively appointed nor are they beholden to recommend what the superordinate expects. Political maneuvering is discouraged in teams. There are some special characteristics of TQE teams, something like athletic teams in the moment of battle. During each play of the game, a football team relies on its own resources, must adjust its directions, and is accountable for its decisions.

TQE teams identify their own focuses; team members select the problems on which they wish to work. They also hold some degree of autonomy relative to the manner in which they operate, in that they select the attacks on the problem, the possible solutions, and the initial implementation of the solution and the tracking of progress. They manage the problem; they control the process. TQE teams also involve everyone on the team and in the organization. Everyone can be a team member in TQ; everyone is given the opportunity to participate. Teams can be homogeneous or heterogeneous. Since they are voluntary they are structured to collect independent thinking on the best way to attain a goal, which they establish. These teams work by consensus only. Quality team behavior is nonthreatening; everyone desires the same end. Quality teams promote an environment for personal growth.

Teams work for several psychological reasons that make them distinct from groups. First, team agendas are legitimate and significant to the participants. Being close to the problem, team members have relevant knowledge and skills that create personal relevance and motivation. Second, the fact that a person is a member of an identified team rewards ego needs and promotes a sense of self-importance. Third, team decisions are team products and give the feeling of contributing to a joint effort. Pride and self-actualization are heightened. Fourth, team discussion, problem-solving techniques, and decision process sensitize team members to emerging identities that promote loyalty and sharper levels of commitment. Team decision making helps encourage people to think differently. The interplay of ideas stimulates creativity. Last, team processes finalized by team member public commitment affect subsequent individual behavior and bind the team together.[7]

Teams require training in problem solving, decision making, negotiation and conflict resolution strategies, member roles, and facilitator-leader skills. There is a strong indication that little training has occurred in educational committees, grade-level teams, citizen committees, and task forces in teamwork, team development, team leadership, or problem solving. Educational groups assume they already have the training to make them effective. The popular notion that each member has as much to contribute as another is somewhat true. But groups with varied individual training do not usually tap the potential of the members who have less training or lower self-esteem. There is little attempt in these kinds of groups to use formalized problem-solving tools other than brainstorming. There is usually heavy emphasis on individual subjective experiences or feelings. The best example of this is what is happening in Kentucky where there has been almost no training of site-based management groups mandated by the Kentucky Education Reform Act. These groups not only lack team training but also the team problem-solving skills necessary to be functionally effective.

Teams are not something that just rise up and flower somewhat like the character of administratively appointed groups. Teaming takes a newer style of leadership, emphasizing such skills and roles as team building, vision exemplar, resource generator, and change agent. The new team leader is a process observer, patient enough to allow teams to develop in their own time. Team members need time for orientations and development of structures and roles, and time to learn to be a team before they finally collaborate into team work.

Teaming requires rewards for success. Few educational groups seem to have received much more than their own organic satisfaction for a job well done. TQM teams are motivated partly by recognition and rewards. It is acceptable practice in successful TQ organizations to tie a valued reward to a performance the teams believe to be achievable. Gain sharing and profit sharing are acceptable practices in business. In TQE enterprises, the quality improvement council is responsible for the assurance of suitable incentives, recognition, rewards celebration, and financial gain for teams and individuals. Currently very little of this exists in public education. Is there a difference between education groups and TQE teams?

Commitment to Self-Management and Leadership

Self-determination is an American principle. Business is learning that the desire to self-actualize is strong within everyone whose basic needs have been met. If this desire is not acted out at work, it is acted out away from work. Why not allow people some opportunity to determine more about their jobs, more about the future of their business, and more about satisfying their customers? Why not allow people the opportunity to control and own more of their workday achievement? All of this begins with a belief that individuals can and do make a difference! TQ organizations are finding that all people given basic training have valuable input to quality improvements, even the least educated and the least paid. Time and time again hospitals find orderlies with sophisticated and sensitive solutions to complicated problems; factories find custodians with practical design and operational improvement ideas. If this is so, schools will find bus drivers with practical solutions to recruiting and instructional problems. TQ organizations practice the belief that everyone has potential to contribute in many ways to the organization. The key to unlock the potential of others is through the unlocking of personal beliefs, expectations, values, and attitudes through opportunities for personal growth. Everyone in schools must believe in the power of the human mind, the boundlessness of the human spirit, and the ability to change our performance and our environment. Everyone must believe that people can manage themselves and work toward expecting that of everyone.

Positive self-management begins with a consistent philosophy in the organization. An effective TQ organization takes time to organize itself so that all efforts lead to the external customer. It determines clear statements of their mission, guiding principles, customer focus strategy, and goals and objectives that are agreed on from the bottom up. These are reflected in the tasks decided, the technologies selected, and the facilities designed. The structure of the system allows operating personnel to manage and have input into organization wide strategic planning, information, and decision-making processes. People are empowered through systematic consistent processes included in recruiting, selection, orientation, training, certification, performance goal setting, and career development. A reward system is in place and it works. An organizational renewal process works not only to evaluate the organization but to determine strategies for improvement. The organization exhibits these things in its style of leadership, beliefs, and values. Once the organization knows and can tell others where it is going, people can manage themselves within it.

Self-management also requires that individuals be taught to understand how the human mind operates to achieve a quality performance. This not only includes positive and possibility thinking, but positive self-talk, mental discipline, and a realization that we can control our performance and environment. Everyone needs to know what goal setting is and how the goal-setting principle operates organically as a motivator and how visualization affects behavior. Everyone must learn that each of us is accountable for our own decisions and that we choose to do or not to do things for our own reasons. As Tice says, "All meaningful and lasting change starts first on the inside of us and works its way out."[8] Self-management can be learned in phases, by all of us. We have been taught in so many ways to be dependent on *other-management* (other people controlling us) that many of us will have a difficult time "wanting" to manage ourselves.

For many organizations it will take a great deal of discipline to identify the organizational design containing the mission, guiding principles, customer focus strategy, goals, and objectives, and their reflection in the organization. This in itself will take constructive group leadership. Managers who only plan and organize to direct and control people, with styles that rely on "command" mixed with "consult," will struggle with the consensus style of new group leadership. They will need special training and support to believe that what they have always been doing is not altogether wrong but needs improvement.

Constructive group leadership depends on facilitative leader behaviors, those that make it easier for others to do things right by themselves. Facilitators are helpers, not directors. They encourage individuals and teams to solve their own problems. Facilitators are concerned about group process, about how people are behaving, and about how things are working between people. Facilitators are team-oriented; the group is product-oriented. They are expert questioners, encouraging multiple answers from multiple thinkers. They display positive regard and trust in people and encourage others to do the same. They understand why people do as they do and use motivational techniques to satisfy the drives within people. Facilitators share the highest expectations, knowing that people need to achieve. They believe and act knowing that ownership of processes, problems, products, and programs is key to success. Constructive leaders command only in emergencies. Good leaders remember that they themselves can become the focus of others' energies if they use directive behaviors. They know that this behavior restricts group potential because individuals then work for the leader rather than the customer. An effective facilitator is not an obstacle in the road but a road crew to clear the road. Good leaders wish for their teams to make their own decisions and expect them to share their successes and failures. Good leaders celebrate with them when they succeed and commiserate with them when they fail. To a good leader, there is only one kind of management, self-management.

Commitment to Continual Improvement

Use of the PDSA cycle ensures continual improvement. The PDSA cycle relies on more than perceptions and intuition. Team problem solving with data replaces what I have seen in many organizations as a PUMP effort (pushing up more pneumatics). This effort at problem solving is characterized by temporary emotional excitement about a problem, quick decisive planning for a solution, and often little follow through because other problems come up that seem bigger than the first problem. PUMP efforts are more air than substance. Individual perception causes a PUMP effort. As often as not, intuition is the major factor in solution identification. The PDSA cycle requires team understanding, acceptance, willingness to be owner, and committed planning based on data and prediction as well as action toward team goals and celebration of achievement. A good explanation of the PDSA cycle is given in Figure 5.1.

Continual improvement will depend on use of the tools of quality. Application of the PDSA cycle in all improvement efforts forces

Plan	Monitor and access performance.	Review process history.
		Are objective and subjective data available?
		Develop and apply data-gathering schemes.
		Sketch existing process through checklists, flow charts, and control charts.
		Ask if trends are getting worse or better.
	Plan alternatives.	Brainstorm. Use fishbone diagrams. Plan pilot. What is best scale, how long trial?
		Inform affected internal customers.
Do	Do trials.	Gather facts, objective and subjective; survey observers and participants.
		Keep trial short and small, coach participants about trial, be available during trial to discuss.
Study	Study results.	Develop why-why and fishbone diagrams; get input on results, behaviors.
		Can future results, behaviors be predicted?
Act	Take action.	Abandon trial. Why?
		Run trial under new terms.
		Adopt plan, coach, and train those involved.
		Develop controls, measure benefits. What was learned?
		What is to be done next?

Figure 5.1   The Continuous Improvement Process

people to slow down, be methodical, and put their thinking and actions into sequence. It ensures consistent application of action, based on study results with team perceptions of both intuition and experience with the reinforcement of data. Professional educators have always believed in continual improvement; they just haven't had the tools to attain their visions. The PDSA cycle with the tools of quality is such a tool.

Some schools in Alaska, Pennsylvania, and New York are applying some of the tools of quality for school improvement. At Mt. Edgecumbe High School in Sitka, Alaska, teacher-student teams have collected sample data of what is going on in the classroom and work together to improve instruction, student attendance, and other concerns in what the school calls a continuous improvement process. In the Crawford Central School District in Meadville, Pennsylvania, maintenance problems are quantified using control charts and approached through team efforts. The George Westinghouse Vocational and Technical School in Brooklyn, New York, is working on achievement through the use of Shewhart thinking—data collection, analysis, and doing some-thing about the data.[9]

Commitment to Belief in Individual and Team Potential

The quality game is played in many modes—singles, doubles, and total teams—but everyone is a contributing member and every-one can be a coach. One obstacle to improvement in America is the great number of traditional coaches who believe they are the only ones who can call the plays. These command coaches can't trust teams to call their own plays: "They are just cannons to be fired at my signal." These so-called cannons usually are earnest workers seeking improvement through self-determination. Because some managers are not disciplined enough or wise enough to determine a structure of empowerment for others, they see their job as captain of the ship. This management style fails to see individuals and teams as people with creative minds. Collectively, this brain power is far more capable than one captain.

Children, youths, and adults can often learn and do more than the current education system allows. The learning management style in many schools today is a "control" system, much like smokestack management. It ties initiative down tightly and binds teachers and learners to management determinations rather than self-determinations. This style is much like steering a sailboat into the wind. The captain and crew can work with the wind and tack together, or they can lay anchor and wait until the wind is in their favor. The captain with the most competence learns to sail the ship with the help of the crew using the wind for their own direction. Quality ships have "captains," but the crew helps chart the course and sail the ship. The captain must rely on the crew for more than physical labor or menial tasks.

TQ is a different way of thinking. It is thinking that others *can* do. It is thinking that many minds make better decisions than one mind. It is knowing that people will improve quality better if given a chance. It is believing as a leader that much of the problem in the organization has to do with the way management behaves. It is believing that, as a leader, you can develop a championship team no matter who the players are, because you really know how to get them to perform their best by getting them to think their best. It is knowing that it is mankind's task to improve human conditions.[10]

Commitment to Quality

Quality means meeting the requirements of the customer. Quality is improving human conditions. It ought to be a concern to our nation, which espouses human rights and the improvement of the human condition, to be outdone by other nations' efforts in these arenas. It should bother Americans tremendously to be known among other nations as a nation which has apparent ideals about improving the human condition but which favors first the accumulation of physical goods. It ought to sadden our people to know that we have blinded ourselves by the number of things in our lifestyle rather than the excellence in them. The fact that an entire generation of Americans has grown up to believe that the spirit and product of goodness has been based on deception about the quality of products and the manipulation of minds through advertising should stir us to improvement. We must become alert to what so many Americans and others believe about our products and services: "They don't last." "They don't work." "They cost too much."

Educators have known about these same faults in the educational system. But few external customers really listened. Few outside the schools supported or involved themselves in the change for improvement in schools. It seemed no one else really cared except educators. Few at the local level understood the call for improvement in the 1960s. Few outside the schools cared about the loss of productivity of the 1970s. The external customer called business finally cried for help in the 1980s when business learned that the quality of American education affected the economy for good or ill. Most states responded with top-down driven reform regardless of the educational process or what we knew about schools and learning. The 1990s will see a big government, big business, and flurry of ideas, innovations, and external dollars to incite change in education. All of this lacks the reasonable approach to quality improvement inherent in a systematic TQ process. Human beings must understand the problem, be close to it, and have the will to solve it. People solve problems one at a time, by themselves, at their own pace. "All meaningful and lasting change starts first on the inside and works its way out."[11]

Summary

A Declaration of TQE embraces seven principles found in TQ programs around the world. They include:

1. Total management commitment—if educational leaders aren't committed, TQE can't happen.

2. Customer first focus, always—like good educators who believe the child comes first, TQE requires that internal and external customers come first.

3. Commitment to teamwork—using true problem-solving techniques with teams of concerned, trained people who challenge problems.

4. Commitment to self-management and leadership—everyone must learn, believe, and behave knowing that people can eventually manage themselves. Self-determination is not limited to managers alone. A new leadership is required in TQE.

5. Commitment to continuous improvement—kaizen in American terms means using the PDSA cycle on everything.

6. Commitment to believe in individual and team potential—all processes, services, and requirements.

7. Commitment to quality—means helping others.

Notes

1. Encyclopaedia Brittanica. *Total Quality Control Pocket Guide*. Encyclopaedia Brittanica Educational Corporation, Chicago, 1990.

2. Ronald H. Axtell and Starr L. Eckholdt. *Organizational Systems Design*. RHA and SEA Inc., Salt Lake City, 1989, ch. 1, p. 35.

3. Committee for Economic Development. *Investing in Our Children*. Research and Policy Committee of the Committee for Economic Development, New York, 1985, p. 5.

4. Anthony P. Carnevale and Leila J. Gainer. *The Learning Enterprise*. American Society for Training and Development, U.S. Department of Labor, Washington, D.C., 1990, p. 19.

5. Grady Regas. "Leading to Excellence." American Society for Training and Development presentation, Knoxville, November 1990.

6. James A. Belasco. "Empowering Others." National Park Service management presentation, Atlanta, 1990.

7. Ned Rosen et al. *Teamwork and the Bottom Line*. Lawrence Ehrlbaum and Associates, Hillsdale, N.J., 1989, pp. 177–178.

8. Lou Tice. "Investments in Excellence." Videotape. The Pacific Institute, Seattle, 1986.

9. Tricia Kelly. "Elementary Quality." *Quality Progress* (October 1991): 51–56.

10. Lou Tice. "Strategic Thinking, Strategic Planning." Videotape. The Pacific Institute, Seattle, 1990.

11. Lou Tice. "Investments in Excellence." Videotape. The Pacific Institute, Seattle, 1986.

Chapter 6
A Plan for Implementation
in the Public Schools

"I plan to spend the rest of my life in the future, so I want to be reasonably sure of what kind of future it's going to be. That is my reason for planning."

Charles Kettering

Critical Mass Development

Efforts in implementing TQM require a plan. The PDSA cycle should be the model for such an enterprise. The PDSA cycle ensures awareness of the participants, ownership by them, a structure to follow, a process for implementing pilots, and a pivotal point for review and recycling. A plan is necessary to increase the critical mass of people who understand, accept, and use the information.

Expanding the critical mass of participants is key to the success of the process. This new information will be frightening to people because it involves change—change in thinking—and change in behavior. Any plan for TQ implementation must include strong components for awareness and ownership. Awareness means helping people understand the concept and the new economy. Ownership means allowing people to find personal and local reasons for the need for change.

Top-down quality improvement efforts, like accreditation efforts in schools, may have people going through the motions, but they may lack the ownership (the personal buy-in) of each individual in the total organization. The efforts may wind up with recommendations for improvement according to the guidelines required; the schools may win the accreditation. Some hospital services and businesses, too, may have won accreditation or awards in a similar manner, but in either case do they win the customer? Accreditation agencies suggest that they only require the conditions for excellence. It is up to everyone in the school to require behavioral excellence.

The Baldrige and Deming awards processes are at least as thorough as school accreditation processes which are also based on criteria. Some businesses, after years of implementation of TQM and a Baldrige or Deming review, have learned of the lack of total employee ownership of quality processes in the company. This is sometimes due to the deployment of TQ or the driving of the program mostly by management. There is no doubt that the accreditation or the award is valuable; but in some cases, it rather than the customer may become the goal. People will generally do what is expected, whether it is to do their job, to meet the standards of accreditation, or to fulfill the criteria for an award or a customer.

Before the First Step

Frederick Smith of Federal Express says it this way: "Respect for the dignity of our people demands that we answer some simple and universal questions: What do you expect of me? What's in it for me? Where do I go with a problem?"[1] These are basic questions to answer before beginning a TQ plan. Administration must answer these questions before it begins implementing TQ. According to Smith, the answers are as follows: "First, do your job as clearly defined and trained for. Second, expect an increase in pride, satisfaction in your job, and financial rewards. Third, go with a problem to your team, to your superordinate, or if necessary, to the appeals process."[2]

A good TQ plan will be proactive to clearly define everyone's role and to recognize people for quality improvement achievements. A good plan will ensure that information access and work environments are open and trusting, so that everyone can become a problem solver. The builders of the plan will keep in mind that the development of a critical mass is the key to success.

Additional cautions should be mentioned for successful accomplishment of the plan. Consider first that the pace of implementation is relative to the readiness of the participants. Start at the top and start small. Begin with a department or grade. Ensure that they are totally with you and have bought in to the plan. Ensure their success through training and mentoring. It may take three to five years or longer to achieve TQ.

An excellent method to develop awareness and general participation is to do an organizational assessment using a survey instrument of all persons in the department or school. Instruments exist that determine the perception of participants about leadership of the quality effort, information and analysis of the information, strategic planning, quality assurance and quality results of products and services, and customer and stakeholder satisfaction. This survey information can become not only an awareness tool but baseline data collection for future use.

Second, believe that ownership and understanding are more important than quick results. The temptation will be to prove to yourself and others that TQ works. Once people realize what you are talking about, there is enough common sense in TQ that people will want to take initiative. The great task will be to mentor them into correct, patient action.

Third, believe that as people understand the process and you mentor them along, results will occur exponentially. People as owners will sell the process to others as they see results. This kind of awareness sharing is probably more important than awareness sessions. Training needs to occur at the teachable moment, not before. The teachable moment is when people need the knowledge. One of the big mistakes in business has been to think that everyone must know statistical process control even if they don't use or understand it. Be aware that there are people within your school who can train others—people you never would have thought were able. Know, too, that training is most needed at the administrative level first.

Fifth, realize that school people are no different than others in relation to rewards and recognition. Educators are giving people, often to the detriment of themselves. Plan for recognition, financial rewards, and celebrations for improvement.

Sixth, structure is important. Training must be structured. There must be a consistent process for identifying quality concerns, allocating resources, forming teams, and implementing and reviewing the system.

Success often breeds success. Be sure that quality improvement efforts are within the abilities and realm of the quality improvement teams. It can be very easy for teams to set goals beyond their ability, resources, or jurisdiction if they are not mentored along well. Successful pilots will ensure a successful process.

TQ in the schools is not a quick fix. It is a process by which people and things will get better, and it will not happen overnight.

About Training Everyone

It may seem odd to emphasize the importance of training to people in the training business. Although TQ may seem passé to many, it does require a change in the educational culture. TQE is a new way of doing things for many people, and this requires training. Training will not only promote new concepts of ways to do things, but it will also identify common terminology for all school people. This common terminology will enhance understanding and communication.

Educators are accustomed to attending courses, classes, and seminars for information or credit. As professional learners they learn easily, and they are adept at sorting out what seems applicable to their lives and what is not. It is important that training be of the highest hands-on caliber and pertinent to the level of learner and the TQ concepts. It is vital that the training be highly organized and professionally presented. It must be timely and pertinent to the "teachable moment." It must be led by someone open to innovative teaching who is knowledgeable of how adults learn. He or she must also understand quality concepts and have a world view of necessary educational improvements rather than a local or regional educational view.

Educators in many ways are futurists and philosophers, so the training must emphasize why, who, what, how, and when all things will happen. The nature of educators requires management to be prepared to answer these questions in the training sessions. Remember that school personnel are customers of the trainers. The broad requirement of these customers is that they must understand, own, and use the information.

Tentative Training Plan

The major goals of the training process should include the following:

1. Understanding and ownership of the process.
2. Knowledge and understanding of the tools for self-management.

3. Opportunities with mentors to apply skills effectively.

4. Perceptions that people and things are better than before.

5. Opportunity and expectation to share successes and to improve all processes.

6. Understanding and use of the tools of quality and the PDSA cycle.

A phased program of training might include the following sequence:

Phase I: Awareness
Why, what of TQE

Phase II: Ownership
External customer service information exchange
Quality audit, quality survey
Internal customer requirements exchange
Information collection, summary, recommendations

Phase III: TQ Structure
Quality council
Improvement priorities
Team development, roles, leadership
PDSA cycle

Phase IV: Problem Solving
Group dynamics
Nonstatistical problem solving
Statistical problem solving
Decision making

Phase V: Investigation of Data
Examining results
Making predictions
Instituting process controls
Initiating pilots

Phase VI: Reviewing and Recycling

Topics for training in sequence include:

Phase I: Awareness (Everyone)
A. State of current education efforts internationally
   1. In major industrialized countries
   2. In third world countries
B. Future business climates
   1. Environment
   2. Demands of infrastructure
   3. Expectations of educated work force
   4. Governmental regulations
   5. Competitive wage rates
   6. Population attitude toward quality
C. Work force of the future
   1. Education
   2. Work habits
   3. Problem-solving ability
   4. Group member relations
   5. Diversity in thought and culture
D. Status of local and state educational efforts
   1. Relative to international
   2. Worst-best scenario for economic future
   3. Longitudinal picture of graduates the last five years
   4. Areas for improvement
E. Expectations of customer and school deficiencies
   1. Basic skills
   2. Attitudes
   3. Thinking skills
   4. Relationships with others
   5. Ability to innovate
   6. Initiative
   7. Will to compete

F. What is TQE?
   1. Definition
   2. Business examples
   3. Shewhart beliefs
   4. Deming beliefs
   5. Customership, internal and external
G. Declaration of TQE
H. Tentative plan

Phase II: Ownership (Everyone)
A. External customer service information exchange
   1. Identification of customers, external and internal
   2. Individual information collection, personal and survey
   3. Information dialogue, reporting
   4. Within the department or school
      a. Within the system
      b. Identification of quality improvement areas
      c. Prioritizing
         1) By department
         2) By council
B. Quality audit
   1. Leadership
   2. Information collection
   3. Human resource utilization
   4. Quality assurance
   5. Quality results
   6. Strategic planning for quality
   7. Customer satisfaction
C. Internal customer requirements exchange
   1. Identification of customers
   2. Individual information collection

3. Information recording and prioritizing
4. Recommendations to administration, consensus
5. Affirmation of service
6. Recommendations, reports to council

Phase III: TQ Structure (Everyone)
A. Quality council
   1. Composition
   2. Responsibilities
      a. Prioritizing improvements
      b. Allocating resources
      c. Training
      d. Recognition, celebration
      e. Mentoring, monitoring
      f. Pacing progress
B. Quality improvement teams
   1. School level
      a. Responsibilities
         1) Codes
         2) Charters
         3) Recommendations to council
         4) Training
         5) Mentoring
         6) Recognizing
         7) Support
   2. Department, grade level
      a. Responsibilities
         1) Problem identification
         2) Team development
         3) PDSA use
         4) Reporting
         5) Training
         6) Recognition

Phase IV: Problem Solving (Selected, Prepared Teams)
A. Group dynamics
    1. Member roles
    2. Collaborative behaviors
    3. Conflict resolution
    4. Consensus decision making
    5. Negotiation
    6. Team leadership responsibilities
    7. Team responsibilities
B. Nonstatistical problem solving
    1. Tools of quality
C. Statistical tools
    1. Histograms, charts
    2. Pareto charts
    3. Run charts
    4. Control charts
    5. Scattergrams

Phase V: Investigation of Data (Selected, Prepared Teams)
A. Examining, comparing data
B. Making predictions from data
C. Instituting process controls
D. Initiating pilots
    1. Responsibilities
    2. Pace
    3. Size
    4. Cost
    5. Reporting results
E. Cost-to-benefit analysis
F. Recycling recommendations

Phase VI: Reviewing and Recycling (Selected, Prepared Teams)

A. Concurrence of school quality improvement team
B. Preparing and working with additional personnel
C. Cost-to-benefit analysis
D. Continuation

Special Responsibilities

School Board and Administration

School leaders should create a solid vision for everyone in the school environment that is flexible and changes in response to parent and educator input. School leaders should responsibly become futurists of the system. This requires that they identify strategies for the short and long terms. Individually each leader should initiate personal efforts to change and improve through study of high involvement management, learning psychology, and modern management psychology. School leaders must begin to realize how important it is to "walk the talk," and align the ideas of self-management with their own behaviors. Leaders need to prepare psychologically for sharing control, delegating more authority, and relying more on others to get things done. They should begin reducing the number of bureaucratic restrictions and policies binding others to homogeneous control.

Additionally, the school board and administration must initiate a quality council to lead the quality effort. The council must provide resources, ensure open information and communications, publicize progress, set priorities for improvement, plan, provide training services, plan the progress of the TQ system, communicate and celebrate successes, and evaluate progress.

Teachers, Department Leaders, and Support Service Supervisors

This group must communicate the board's vision, mission, guiding principles, customer focus strategy, goals, and objectives to everyone. It must work to gain the commitment of everyone with whom it interacts, including parents, students, aides, and support people. It becomes the responsibility of these middle managers to translate organizational design features into functional, useful learning and behavioral strategies and activities. These middle leaders are helpful in synchronizing their own activities and those of others by keeping the vision clear in all minds. They become the communication link between all people for information, reports of progress, and recommendations for improvement. They are the key to focusing on quality improvement through everyday use of the PDSA cycle and the facilitative style. They also must begin to accept the new empowerment to identify, solve, and implement solutions to quality concerns. They must learn and apply the skills of team leader, facilitator, trainer, and participating team member.

Like the administration, all teachers, department leaders, and support service supervisors must begin to think differently about self-management and managing others. They must prepare themselves for change and participation in new ideas wholeheartedly and positively. They should be ready to form varieties of teams of all kinds of members. They must accept the new definition of customer and spread its gospel. They must participate in training with open minds and with active constructive behaviors that will lead to changed attitudes and changed behaviors.

Students must be prepared as early as possible to accept self-management and grow in sequential development of personal responsibility for self-discipline, learning, and collaboration with others. They must be trained in their new responsibilities of inquiring, acquiring, and requiring of themselves and of other people in a positive, respectful, persistent manner. They must be prepared for individual and team activities centered on progressive learning for the sake of personal contribution when they enter the world of careers. All of this is a new emphasis for many students. This emphasis on "personal contribution" may help students realize that they, like all others in the school, are accountable to the community in which they will serve. Students are accountable for their efforts or lack of efforts in gaining what is available to learn and use.

Young people, like everyone else, must learn and use the PDSA cycle. And they should expect all others to use it with them. They should be taught nonstatistical problem solving and, as soon as possible, statistical problem solving. Problem-solving skills should stand them in good stead for personal decision making, team applications, and future learning and careers—and for improving schools.

The concepts of customer service, personal contribution, and meeting customer requirements must be shared extensively with students and all others. Students must realize that their purpose in school is twofold: first, for their own personal development as Americans and as participating community citizens, and second, for the development of the skills to serve others. Currently, success in entertainment, athletics, or business require little education. A completely renewed attitude must be developed about the purpose in life being the service of others. This must be taught in society, and it must be taught at home.

Renewed Accountability

The Newtonian world view with which we have been living for more than 300 years taught us that the universe is a machine. Isaac Newton's views have affected our educational systems, economic systems, and religious and political systems. Part of this view is the perception of the organization with a pyramid structure, where those at the top make the important decisions, and those at the bottom follow orders. In the Newtonian structure, accountability resides at the top.

The Whiteheadian view of this century, that each individual can contribute and control a constructive destiny in the world, indicates a shift from the Newtonian paradigm to a new order. Alfred North Whitehead has invented a world in which each individual is accountable for his or her own thinking and behaviors. The Whiteheadian world is characterized by individual equity and participative creativity through high involvement. Whitehead has reversed the organizational structural pyramid to propose lowest-to-top management rather than top-down management. This style requires accountability from those at the top and those at the bottom. In the Newtonian top-down organizational view, those at the bottom cannot be trusted. The Whiteheadian bottom-up structure assumes a personal trustworthiness and responsibility on the part of everyone to be accountable for his or her own service regardless of place in the organizational structure.[3]

A Plan for Implementation

Phase I: Awareness and Commitment

Aim: To establish board and administration commitment to TQE and to communicate that commitment to the rest of the school organization.

Objectives:

- To communicate, display, and honor the Declaration of TQE
- To model the declaration and become the first to be trained in understanding and application of the declaration
- To identify a physical symbol of the TQE effort, which can be used as an image denoting personal commitment, the school system vision, and the idea of customership
- To share information through additional communication media
- To identify the goals and objectives of years one through three of the program
- To identify a training program with resources, personnel, and support for the entire school system
- To identify a time sequence for implementing the training plan
- To share the philosophy, need, and structure of the TQE system with everyone
- To create a quality council of esteemed persons from all walks of life to mentor and guide the process in all facets

Phase II: Ownership

Aim: To allow everyone the opportunity through voluntary involvement to understand and participate in recognizing the need for TQE.

Objectives:

- To train all personnel in the specifications of external customership and interview techniques
- To promote personalized interviews with external customers, including business, industry, service agencies, higher education, and the military by any school personnel to determine areas for improvement
- To collect and record interview information for reporting, discussion, study, and recommendation to the quality council
- To train all personnel in internal customership and identify requirements
- To promote personalized interviews with all parents to train them and to clarify their responsibilities and to contract them to an affirmation of service
- To identify the internal customer support issues through personal internal customer interviews and recommend these to the quality council for prioritization as internal customer responsibilities
- To create quality improvement councils within each school that will ensure communication, team development, prioritization of projects, and training of personnel in a timely fashion, and that will monitor and publish progress reports, ensure recognition, and consist of varieties of persons
- To develop, survey, and collect data; promote discussion of data and of opinions from school personnel, students, and parents concerning the quality of the school relative to Baldrige or other criteria
- To recommend collected data to the quality and quality improvement councils for priority response and training decisions

Phase III: Organization and Planning

Aim: To create the organization needed to implement quality improvement and to develop plans for continuous improvement at all levels of the education community.

Objectives:

- To organize each level of the school system into quality teams to initiate quality improvement activities and to establish teamwork throughout the schools on a voluntary basis, including all levels of administration
- To develop a team structure that shares decision making by equitable representation of all participants in all councils
- To develop a TQ plan that describes how everyone will be involved at all levels, trains all persons in quality improvement concepts and methods, identifies indicators of quality within the system, implements recognition systems for quality progress, evaluates yearly accomplishments, and develops a renewal plan for all efforts
- To help people perceive the need for self-managed accountability for quality improvement

Phase IV: Implementation

Aim: To develop processes enabling the entire school system to participate in and contribute to quality improvement actively by focusing on the major quality issues of the schools.

Objectives:

- To train teams and other personnel at teachable moments in those subjects required
- To identify quantifiable indicators from the customer requirements as standards for measuring quality improvements

- To begin to perceive behaviors exemplified by the Declaration of TQE
- To involve all levels of the school in quality improvement through individual, team, and heterogeneous group efforts
- To utilize multimedia means to share improvements, innovations, ideas, and general progress
- To increase participation and morale through obvious, declared recognition efforts to stimulate participants
- To ensure input and flexibility in the organization through the practice of the Deming principles

Phase V: Recognition and Renewal

Aim: To provide encouragement, reinforcement, and renewal of the continuing process of quality improvement through development and implementation of systems for recognizing outstanding quality performance by teams and individuals; to provide a continuous cycle of quality training for renewing the school system's commitment to quality education

Objectives:

- To recognize the teams and individuals who participate in quality improvement
- To develop an award structure and recognition process for each level of improvement activities
- To provide a recordable means for easy input to suggest and recognize quality improvement ideas for action
- To publish progress and achievements for recognition and record
- To celebrate achievements
- To identify additional training needs
- To develop a renewal plan for succeeding years based on continual improvement

Getting Started

The implementation of TQ may be informal or formal. Many groups rely on an informal plan known only at the executive level that contains the TQ elements needed and is implemented with no sequence or time structure. With good leadership this plan unfolds as employees are ready or as they identify a need to implement a component without the sophistication of a known plan. Many organizations use this procedure because it reduces the anxiety of change and seems to remake the culture of the organization in a more natural, when-ready phasing process. Many smaller organizations choose an informal procedure because of limited personnel, budget, schedules, and other resources.

Site-Based Management as a Pilot

Site-based management is a term currently used to denote participative decision making utilizing parents, educators, and students at the local school level. This movement is characterized by some degree of autonomy allowed the local school to create and abide by rules, regulations, and policies that may differ from local board of education regulations and policies. These kinds of groups are represented more and more in state education laws and in metropolitan school systems.

Site-based management groups in education are sometimes called instructional improvement councils, school site decision-making councils, or school advisory councils. Their purpose is to support customization of the local school program to support its own particular goals and needs, which may differ from those of other schools and communities. The groups usually are composed of the principal, parents, teachers, local school support persons, sometimes a central office person, and often students in the school. Their focus is often an administratively delegated target to be resolved by the group through committee discussion. These groups have little training in group dynamics, group problem solving, or decision making.

The management of school site units has often been said to be the responsibility of the principal with or without staff or community input. But much of the planning, organizing, staffing, directing, and controlling of local schools is bound by school district or system policy, tradition, or regulation. Managing schools has often become primarily an activity of policy implementation. In other words, principals manage district policy at the local school site. Many of the important activities or decisions about curriculum, textbooks, teacher assignments, instructional strategies, pupil-teacher relationships, staff development, school schedules, or bus schedules are bound by district-wide policies or agreements. Much of the decision making at the local site level revolves around whether or not a proposal fits within district guidelines. The remainder of local site decision making is relegated to items of lesser importance such as recess schedules, lunch and bus duty assignments, adult coverage of athletic contests, extracurricular activity sponsorship, parent-teacher conference dates, student picture schedules, and the local internal funds development festival.

It may be possible to use the current site-based management concept to implement TQE at the local school site. The role of the local site management committee might be redefined as the school quality council. The school quality council could initially implement school site problem solving and decision making as its mode of operation, and eventually expand its success throughout the school by developing successful subcouncils. These subcouncils would focus on member interest activities using group problem-solving and decision-making strategies. Initially, the interests of all the councils would be on quality improvement through effective decision making.

As local site success grows, more and more of the actual responsibility and accountability for school site management—the planning, organizing, staffing, directing, and controlling—might be turned over to the quality councils. The corporate manufacturing world sometimes recognizes this strategy in what is called independent business units.

Business units may be subsidiary plant sites of a corporation that use TQ processes and are accountable for the majority of the management tasks of the business unit. Within corporate guidelines the business unit plans, organizes, staffs, directs, and controls the operations for which it is responsible. Using a lean administrative organization, quality councils, and teams (sometimes self-managing teams), it solves problems and decides about those issues closest to its customers, the development and manufacturing of product, and continual improvement of product. The business unit has limited unit resources and depends on corporate for resources beyond its own budget, which may include human and research resources as well as financial. The business unit is accountable to corporate for internal and external customership satisfaction as well as operational, product, and financial accountability. The organizational design of each unit reflects not only the need to satisfy customers and motivate and satisfy employees but also to please the multiple shareholders of the company. Ultimately, everyone at the plant site is committed to plant success. Communication is superb; involvement is total. Continual improvement is a pervasive culture that drives the success of the business unit. Site-based management in business and schools can work effectively. Site-based management works where the purposes are clear, internal and external roles are defined, limitations are defined, and participants are trained in how to go about their business. The first effort to promote site-based management as a pilot for TQ in schools might be the adoption of a board of education policy that defines members, purposes, and limitations. Here is a draft school board policy to consider.

School Site Quality Improvement

A school principal who has developed a plan for TQE that uses school site problem solving and decision making with his or her faculty and community shall gain their approval and commitment for the local school to participate in school site quality improvement. He or she may recommend to the superintendent and board of education this plan, which shall be based on use of continuous improvement strategies and effective group problem-solving and decision-making methods. This local problem-solving, decision-making team shall be called a school quality council.

The school quality council shall be composed of an equal balance of instructional staff, community representatives, and students. The council shall be no smaller than six members and no larger than nine. Members shall serve two-year terms, conclusively. The superintendent (or his or her designee) shall be an ex officio member who shall provide information and resources to the council and support success of the council. The principal shall be a member of the council.

The chairperson of the school quality council shall be elected at the first meeting by the voting members. Decisions will be based on a consensus decision-making model and on identified rules for order. The council will construct additionally needed teams of similar balance as it sees fit. It will rely on central office personnel and others for resources as decided.

The school quality council will focus on improvement in the quality of school and student performance as required by the state code (or board of education) through group problem solving and decision making. It shall set goals for the school and shall track and measure their progress. It shall pilot and recommend strategies for improvement of all school and student performance indicators and for standardized assessments or others as it determines. It shall determine improvement strategies for pupil attendance, student morale, teacher morale, student dropout, and teacher retention rates.

It shall serve as a school accountability council in monitoring and reporting the instructional performance of the school relative to its customers. It shall report progress annually to the staff, community, and board of education.

It shall abide by all state rules and regulations, state laws, and board of education administrative policies except where identified.

After the principal has gained local support and the board of education has adopted the policy as revised, the school quality council can be identified, its operating procedures can be selected, and its leaders can be trained in the tools of quality and the PDSA cycle. As soon as the team confidence level approaches readiness to be "open for business," a simple audit of customer-related school and student performance problems can be conducted. The council identifies one problem and begins its efforts at identification, definition, data collection, decision making, development of solutions, and implementation of the PDSA cycle. Building on its own success, the council attacks another concern and resolves it. The council's success will lead to invitations to others interested in the processes to form focus quality councils, which may deal with specific concerns at a student level, a teacher unit, a grade level, or a subject area as decided by the focus quality council. The school administration, with the support of the school quality council, trains each new council. The format is repeated until everyone who wants to participate is involved in group problem solving and decision making in continuous school improvement.

Summary

Implementation of TQE can be started simply by working with those people who are ready to participate in an unhurried application of group problem-solving tools. As participants see an unmet desire to improve, administration trains them in TQE concepts.

TQ may be installed through the use of site-based management groups with principal leadership among school personnel and the community, and with board of education support. Application of modules of the training and implementation plan prepares the site-based management problem-solving, decision-making team to concentrate its efforts on school performance or whatever the principal and board decide.

Large school systems that may require a total culture change may need to apply the entire implementation plan, sequenced so that the critical mass develops successfully. A more formal plan is usually chosen by larger groups, such as IBM,[4] because of the difficulty of changing an entire culture within a work force of thousands of people. A clear written plan is recognizably important to large groups so that every individual knows where the organization is going.

This TQE plan is offered for use in either informal or formal procedures. It is a synthesis of many quality improvement systems that currently work for organizations such as the Philips Consumer Electronics Company.[5]

Notes

1. Frederick Smith. "The Human Side of Quality." An address to the National Quality Forum, October 1990.

2. *Ibid.*

3. Lou Tice. "Strategic Thinking, Strategic Planning." Videotape. The Pacific Institute, Seattle, 1988.

4. Ray F. Boedecker. *Eleven Conditions for Excellence: The IBM Total Quality Improvement Process.* American Institute of Management, Boston, 1989.

5. Philips Consumer Electronics Co. "Quality Improvement System." Greenville, Tenn., 1989.

Chapter 7
Quality Initiatives in
the Schools

"Let us train our minds to desire what the situation
demands."

Seneca

External Models and Improvement

At this writing, millionaire Christopher Whittle is sponsoring the
Edison Project. The Edison Project is a search for model schools characterized by innovative, self-funded, cost-effective approaches that
work. The project aspires, through private funding, to find answers that
educate young people in America to the needs of the future. Ideas are
requested from everyone in America. From these, perhaps 200 model
schools will be chosen, implemented, and evaluated.

During the Bush administration, the U.S. Secretary of Education,
Lamar Alexander, lead a thrust called America 2000. This thrust is
now under the umbrella of a nonprofit corporation called the Hudson
Corporation. Part of this vision was the development of a private foundation to support the development of more than 500 innovative schools
in America. These schools would be parceled out to legislative dis-
tricts. These models would represent the best educational solutions
created to educate American children. The conclusion of this effort is
unknown as the Clinton administration confirms its own education
strategies.

The RJR Nabisco Foundation is in its third year of funding a five-
year, $30 million contest. Fifteen schools each year are awarded funds
for innovations that directly affect student performance, hold promise

of quick implementation and possible replication, and achieve measurable results. There are, of course, multiple private local efforts that also intend to improve schools through new programs.

These and many other efforts like them are commendable. Americans will soon have hundreds of appealing education models to choose from to match their specific local problems. These new school solutions may be the learning processes needed to satisfy American customer requirements. They will exemplify some of the answers educators already know about the value of technology in motivation and learning, the need to match learning and teaching styles, the value of customizing teaching and curriculum to individuals, the importance of low teacher-to-pupil ratios, and how greater resources produce better educated youngsters. But many of these models will not address the fundamental lack of local problem identification and local commitment to paying for and improving the quality of schools.

As Americans, we fail more and more to accept the purpose of education; the responsibilities of the participants; what is to be taught and learned; the processes for improvement; and the value of personal service, accountability, and personal achievement. These are the conditions of quality that must first be decided before a local model is built or chosen. Building model schools or programs is the easy part. Gaining local consensus on the conditions of quality is more difficult. And until the local school community agrees on the conditions, no model, innovation, or program will work consistently.

The American education experience of the 1960s was a period of educational innovation, a thrashing out of models all around the country. It was an attempt to produce more scientists, more engineers, more mathematicians—more and better educated thinking Americans able to make good decisions. The efforts were funded with massive federal and private dollars. Schools tried everything from open-space buildings, modular secondary school schedules, independent learning, language laboratories, and nongraded schools to schools without walls. As one representative of a large private foundation said after the sixties were over, "We learned that the only significant consequence was that there were bigger cars in the teachers' parking lot." What seemed to be a bright idea in one educational community eventually failed for lack of local support in that same community. The variation in belief in the local school community about what makes up the business of schools killed the models. In Shewhart's words, "We cannot have facts without theory." In Deming's words, "People who have no theory don't know where they are going." The local theory must be developed before the model.

It's not a question of treating schools as though they are a business. We already know that American business has not been working as well as it could. It is a question of applying problem solving, commitment development, and philosophy to the improvement of schools. Shewhart and Deming were concerned about "how and what people thought about." Shewhart is telling us that how we think allows us to predict the future. Deming is telling us that it is important for people to be self-determined, to think in groups, and to think within a system. For local school communities it is a question of accepting a local philosophy that helps them improve how everyone thinks.

With all the new models about to be announced in the next several years, it seems reasonable that local school participants should agree on the conditions for quality schools. Once consensus is achieved about the business of schools, a model can be selected that fits their theory. There will never be a model that fits all Americans. Models should fit local, cooperatively accepted theories. TQE proposes such a theory. The Declaration of TQE can be the theory, the education foundation if accepted locally, for the choice of a Whittle, Hudson, or Nabisco model. The problem is not in the model, however, but in the identification of the quality conditions, the principles, and the philosophy espoused by the local school community.

Need for Local Commitment

America lacks an awareness of personal role models that are exemplary of educational success. Many of the people admired in America—those who earn the largest salaries and are national heroes to our youth—are often the least educated. Entertainers, athletes, and entrepreneurs too often share the fact that their success didn't come from education. Their poor language usage and lack of personal self-management are obvious to even the youngest child.

State and federal governmental leaders, both executive and legislative, also lack the luster attributable to making education vital. In too many cases where state spending has exceeded the state budget, education has become important because it becomes the vehicle through which to raise new revenue. Citizens know that lotteries, income taxes, and sales tax increases for the cause of education will soon not be enough to fund all the unannounced government spending.

Education is not and has not been the priority of the federal government. The continual increase of the federal debt suggests that our leaders cared nothing about the future of American children. The entire deregulation debacle that funded the poor practices of bad business emphasizes that quality education isn't even a secondary concern. Additionally, most parents see little federal contribution to their children's education except for occasional special dollars.

If education is to be effective, it must become a local concern. The best role models for youth can be neighbors, families, and others from the community. The resourcefulness and legislation to improve schools can best come from local levels where citizens have some control. It is at the local level where citizens can see and measure educational contributions, and where they can have personal impact. (Maybe this is where the federal and state government can make a difference, by funding local heroes who need help to solidify community sentiment.) This makes it all the more important that a problem-solving commitment strategy be available for local educational communities. For in the end, local schools will invent their own futures, solve their own problems, no matter what the Whittles, Alexanders, or Nabiscos suggest. Like local public services of all sorts, they will have to control and own their education processes.

Improvement Through Local Commitment

The initiatives suggested here are simply possible starting points in the implementation of TQE. The tasks selected are relative to each participating team's responsibility in managing TQE. It is important to remember that the Declaration of TQE, affirmations of service, and the PDSA cycle are key tactics in school quality improvement. The examples chosen are purposefully sequenced in priority of importance for TQE to succeed, in calendar order, and in communication and information value to the whole organization. The sequence begins with the board of education.

Identifying the Requirements for Customer Satisfaction

Plan. The board of education members personally form a team composed of themselves, identify a leader and recorder, and begin to *identify the problem* of customer satisfaction. They might brainstorm and ask, "Who are the customers of our graduates?" They might *define the problem* by focusing on just one type of school customer and where the customer exists; for example, retail services in the community. Their next step is to *investigate the problem* to collect data and facts for more information. It may seem appropriate to survey the major customers in retail services. If so, the board members interview customers. They might use focus groups, mailed surveys, or personal interviews, but they should record the information. Sample questions follow:

1. What percent of our graduates applying to you are qualified for vacant positions? Why do you think this is so?

2. What are the strengths of our graduates that you have hired? Their weaknesses?

3. What specifically, academically and aptitudinally, do you expect of our graduates?

4. How could we improve our graduates for your customer delight?

5. Do you ever see us respond positively about negative feedback that you give us about our graduates?

6. How can we improve that?

7. What should we teach additionally to serve you better?

8. Will your expectations of us be different five years from now? Ten years? Fifteen years? How?

9. What are you willing to teach our graduates after you employ them?

10. How will you commit yourself to participating in TQE in our educational community?

Do. Once these data are collected from the various majority organizations accepting your graduates, the data need to be *analyzed.* A Pareto chart or histogram can be developed and then shared with everyone in the schools. Analysis of the problems continues until priorities surface to the team's perception. The next step is to *solve the problem* through brainstorming, cause-and-effect diagrams, why–why charts, reverse fishbones (reverse cause-and-effect diagrams), and the involvement of educators, parents, and others. As the team finds consensus on the priorities, it sets a goal and a plan to resolve the problem. Then the team puts the plan into action on a small scale and tracks its progress.

Study. Through tracking of the pilot, the team members collect more data about the weaknesses and strengths of the experiment. The data are collected and reviewed, and the team decides, "Is the problem being fixed or not?" "Can it stay fixed with this solution or not?" "Why?" "How?"

Act. The team then revises, expands, or contracts the pilot and continues tracking, measuring, and displaying progress.

Plan. The team continues its efforts with the pilot and possibly goes on to the next prioritized customer's requirements.

By now the board has everyone aware of its efforts, and many others are thinking about who the customer is and what is needed for his or her satisfaction. Because the board members have committed to the Declaration of TQE, they are open to suggestions and solutions from others, and they bring them to the team for consideration. Everyone is watching the board's progress. Possibly for the first time ever, teachers, parents, citizens, students, and the entire school community are learning that the board is truly committed to school improvement. Each board member has gotten involved physically and mentally, and the results are *confirmed.*

Internal Customer Satisfaction

Plan. As modeled by the board of education, the administration now forms a team. This team is composed of interested volunteers from a wide segment of internal customers of the education community who are interested in specifying the requirements of internal customers in the fourth grade. To control efforts in the process, administration determines that it will begin with internal customers who are fourth-grade teachers and one parent from each fourth-grade room. The team meets and chooses a leader and recorder. The members *identify the problem:* "What are the internal customer requirements of participants in the fourth grade?" Through brainstorming, or a why–why diagram or flow chart, they identify the internal customers. They accept as their first concern that parents serve teachers and teachers serve students. They *define the problem,* deciding that parents and teachers have always assumed the requirements of each other. They determine a list of possible requirements for both customers and create a checklist of the requirements through brainstorming. They *investigate the problem* by collecting facts from other parents and teachers in the fourth grade using the checklist. They create histograms and Pareto charts to indicate common priority internal customer requirements. They *analyze the information* individually and together as a team. They determine that there are seven major requirements for parents and eight for teachers that are extremely important. This information is made public. The team decides then to set a goal and develop a plan to *solve the problem,* which can be tracked, measured, and displayed. They invent a pilot solution; it involves six parents from each class and will last 30 days. Administration concurs.

Do. The experiment is launched; the team tracks its progress, measuring and displaying data. Because administration has committed to the Declaration of TQE, administration is doing the book work.

Study. After one month, the team meets, analyzes the evidence collected so far, and shares it with the school's community. The team decides its solution is having a positive impact on student behavior and expanded comfort between parents and teachers. Its results are *confirmed.*

Act. The team decides to expand the pilot to six more parents. Data are collected on all the parents and teachers involved, and the improvement continues.

Plan. When all the fourth-grade teachers and parents have contracted their internal customer requirements, the administration arranges a celebration. Parents and teachers are honored with "customer first" pins, teachers are treated to a restaurant lunch during school lunchtime, and parents receive a coupon for a half gallon of ice cream.

Product and Vendor Specification Initiative

Plan. The purchasing department forms a team of buyers, custodians, a principal, a student, and a product vendor concerning the removal of scuff marks from the gym floor. The team *identifies the problem* through brainstorming as a product quality problem; no solvent currently does the job easily. Using checksheets the team members *define the problem* more clearly and break the problem down to smaller parts through the use of the cause-and-effect diagram. They select a major scuff mark type and *investigate the problem* using a checklist to record the number, time periods, and frequency of a particular type of scuff mark. They *analyze the problem* individually and collectively and learn enough to identify some solutions and characteristics of the product they need. They decide to request samples of products containing certain solvents learned from their analysis by means of the trial use.

Do. They plan a pilot on the gym floors in one building and in several voluntary buildings willing to participate for 60 days. They set goals relative to their desired solution and begin the experiment, tracking, measuring, and displaying the results. They keep the school community informed.

Study. After 60 days the team meets to *confirm* the results. The team members decide by consensus vote that bids should go out for a product of their specifications. They believe they have discovered a solution that meets their requirements.

Act. They purchase product as previously described from one vendor and share it with the pilot schools, but other schools are now interested. The team suggests that if the new buildings will track and report use and progress of the product they too can use it.

Plan. All buildings use the new product, and track and report its value. The head custodian who brought up the problem hosts a soda and popcorn party during lunchtime to celebrate the success. The principals announce the names of their custodians and others over the public address system, thanking them for their help.

Homework Improvement Initiative

Plan. School policy determined by teachers years ago dictates that student homework shall be designed to reinforce daily lessons, promote independent study, prepare for new information, and review for assessment activities. Seven parents in one neighborhood who attend the same church suspect that children are spending an inordinate amount of their time at home studying for tests. It seems that other homework activities are forgotten. The group decides to *identify the problem* through brainstorming. The group participants list the activities the children are assigned. They *define the problem* through a cause-and-effect diagram and determine that the same teachers seem to be at fault. They *investigate the problem* by collecting more data. They keep a checksheet on the kinds of homework assignments made for 10 days. They collect the data and *analyze* it, finding that students spend 80 percent of their time studying for tests.

Do. The parent team prepares its information clearly so the principal and teachers understand. The participants request a meeting with the teachers to share the information. This expanded team brainstorms some solutions. They decide to make balanced assignments throughout the week but to include small amounts of time for studying for tests on a daily basis. They agree to the *solution.* They set a goal and determine a plan, and each parent agrees to continue to track homework assignments.

Study. At the end of 14 class days, the team meets to *confirm* the results of the experiment. The team publishes the results. The plan seems to be working. Most parents are finding improved student habits, which may be due to parent-teacher teaming.

Act. The parents suggest that the Parent Teacher Organization (PTO) might be interested in the process used to resolve this concern. The team chooses representatives to explain the process to other parents and teachers. Some teachers desire more information and want to try the process on other concerns relative to students and parents.

Plan. The process is reviewed with a team from the PTO and discussed as it is implemented and watched by more interested parents and teachers.

A Student Initiative

The board of education has concluded the identification of the external customer requirements and has shared the information with everyone. The administration has drafted these into curricular competencies and graduation requirements for each grade level. Teachers, parents, and students have copies of their grade level and the next grade level competencies. Students clearly know that it is their responsibility to inquire into these competencies, acquire them, and require their exposition in the school. Everyone knows and expects this to be taught during school time.

Plan. The student council of the high school finds that some students believe that not all the competencies of their grade level are not being taught. The council requests volunteer students, teachers, parents, and an administrator to *identify the problem* in a quality improvement project, the focus having been identified by the school quality improvement council. Nine representatives of a suspected grade level form a team and accept responsibility to *define the problem.* The team members choose a leader and recorder. By brainstorming they choose the major topical competencies appearing to be omitted. Using a why–why chart they identify specific teachers who seem to be selectively teaching the competencies. They *investigate the problem* by using checksheets for the next two weeks to identify the amount of time spent on the missing competencies in each class period with the suspected teachers. They collect the data and decide to build a control chart to reflect who taught what during the two weeks. The team meets to review and *analyze* the data.

Do. The team proposes some *solutions.* The team members pick one by a multi-voting technique. They intend to solve the problem by making the teachers aware of what is happening. After administrator preparation of the teachers, the team meets with them to discuss the best plan.

Study. The team continues to use control charts on the progress of the teachers. The charts are reviewed for improvement on a weekly basis for a month with the same first checklist students. The data are *confirmed* that the competencies are being taught. This information is shared with the school community.

Act. The team congratulates the teachers and celebrates its efforts with notes of appreciation to each teacher involved. Copies are sent to the school principal. The principal reports this effort to the school board in a public meeting, congratulating the students for their concern and effort.

Plan. The student council meets again to share with students the progress and the process and to ask if there are other similar concerns in other grades. Some students enter an affirmative answer. The council launches again.

Quality Initiatives Are Those Closest to the Customer

Quality initiatives in the schools may be identified by anyone in the education community. If a quality improvement structure is determined, then concerns will flow through the structure. If there is no structure, then interested persons can seek additional team members, preferably from a variety of roles within the community, and initiate team problem solving. They must use the declaration, the affirmation of service, and PDSA cycle, and maintain an openness about their activities. Support from administration in the form of a charter, a written testimony of support, is necessary,

Suggestions used by others as quality initiatives:

- Student initiatives for time allocations for class length
- Parent initiatives for identifying related home experiences to the curriculum
- Teacher initiatives to develop training teams for all publics of the school
- Teacher initiatives to relate learning styles to teaching styles
- Teacher initiatives to make in-service more customized and useful
- Board initiatives in harvesting private enterprise ideas for school improvement
- Purchasing department vendor certification initiatives
- Family learning projects related to classroom studies
- Teacher, student, and parent self-esteem initiatives
- Custodial service initiatives in environmental health improvement
- Bus driver route scheduling initiatives
- Bus driver student attendance recording initiative
- Staff morale initiatives
- Overall school progress initiatives
- Dropouts and college entrants initiatives

Summary

Public schools must focus on problem solving and commitment at the local level. Once problems have been clearly identified and solutions proposed, then models can be selected to carry out the solutions. Experience has shown that models implemented without local commitment have little chance of success. There has been little ownership of the problem so there has been less ownership of model solutions. Ownership is critical to success.

Quality initiatives should include participants with a variety of perspectives and beliefs. Any educational community member may initiate efforts. Teams should be representative of the multiple publics within the school or education community. Prior to anyone being involved in TQE improvement, he or she must be trained in quality improvement principles.

The quality in education movement continues to progress. To some in education it is just another educational trend. To others, it is a new chance to restructure, reform, and renorm education to make public education all that so many know and believe it can be. Total quality as a term will pass away, but the principles on which it is based will endure. The movement to adopt quality in the public sector is growing. At this writing, Deming is giving his first seminar just for educators. States like New York are giving recognition to school systems which comply with TQ criteria. Review of New York's standards for The Governor's Excelsior Award will indicate the similarity between Excelsior and Baldrige. There's a cultural transformation going on in America, and TQE is part of it. Come join the effort.

Bibliography

Alexander, C. Philip. "Who Is Your Customer?" Communiqué of the Human Resources Division. Milwaukee: ASQC, Vol. 6, No. 3 (September 1990).

Amber, R. W. and H. B. Dull. *Closing the Gap: The Burden of Unnecessary Illness.* New York: Oxford Press, 1987.

American Society for Training and Development. "The New American Economy." *Training* (November 1989): 2.

Axtell, Ronald H. and Starr L. Eckholdt. *Organizational Systems Design.* Salt Lake City: RHA and SEA Inc., 1989.

Belasco, James A. *Teaching the Elephant to Dance: The Manager's Guide to Empowering Change.* New York: Crown Publishers, 1990.

Boedecker, Ray F. *Eleven Conditions for Excellence: The IBM Total Quality Improvement Process.* Boston: American Institute of Management, 1989.

Carnevale, Anthony P. and Leila J. Gainer. *The Learning Enterprise.* Washington, D.C.: American Society for Training and Development and U.S. Department of Labor, 1990.

Committee for Economic Development. *Investing in Our Children.* New York: Research and Policy Committee of the Committee for Economic Development, 1985.

Crosby, P. *Quality Is Free.* New York: McGraw-Hill, 1979.

Davidow, William H. and Bro Uttal. *Total Customer Service: The Ultimate Weapon.* New York: Harper and Row, 1989.

Deming, W. Edwards. *Out of the Crisis.* Cambridge: Massachusetts Institute of Technology, 1986.

De Witt, Karen. "In Vermont Schools, Test on How Well Students Think Draws New Interest." *New York Times,* August 31, 1991, p. 4.

Dobyn, Lloyd. "Ed Deming Wants Big Changes, and He Wants Them Fast." *Smithsonian* (August 1990): 74–82.

Encyclopaedia Britannica. *Total Quality Control Pocket Guide.* Chicago: Encyclopaedia Britannica Education Corporation, 1990.

Fitzgerald, Michael. *Highly Educated, Multi-Skilled People.* Seattle: The Pacific Institute, 1988.

Garfield, Charles. *Peak Performers: The New Heroes of American Business.* New York: Avon Books, 1986.

Harrington, H. James. *The Quality/Profit Connection.* Milwaukee: ASQC Quality Press, 1989.

Imai, K. *Kaizen.* New York: McGraw-Hill, 1986.

Kelly, Tricia. "Elementary Quality." *Quality Progress* (October 1991): 51–56.

Lawler, Edward E. *High Involvement Management.* San Francisco: Jossey-Bass, 1988.

Lipman, M., A. M. Sharpe, and F. S. Oscanyan. *Philosophy in the Classroom.* Upper Montclair, N.J.: Institute for the Advancement of Philosophy for Children, 1977.

Massachusetts School Board Association. "Trends, Guaranteed Graduates." *School Board News* (January 1991): 1.

Naisbitt, John and Patricia Aburdene. *Reinventing the Corporation.* New York: Warner Books, 1985.

Nordstrom Inc. "Nordstrom Employee Handbook." Seattle, 1988.

Papert, Seymour. *Mindstorms: Children, Computers and Powerful Ideas.* New York: Basic Books, 1980.

Perkins, D. M. *The Mind's Best Work.* Cambridge: Harvard University Press, 1981, p. 197, 198, 214–219.

Philips Consumer Electronics Co. "Quality Improvement System." Greenville, Tenn., 1989.

Rosen, Ned. *Teamwork and the Bottom Line.* Hillsdale, N.J.: Lawrence Ehrlbaum and Associates, 1989.

Schoenfeld, Alan H. "Presenting a Strategy for Indefinite Integration." *American Mathematics Monthly* (August 1978): 85–88.

Senge, Peter M. *The Fifth Discipline: The Art and Practice of the Learning Organization.* New York: Doubleday, 1990.

Shewhart, W. A. *Economic Control of Quality of Manufactured Product.* New York: Macmillan-Van Nostrand, 1931. Reissued by ASQC, Milwaukee, 1980.

Sloan, M. Daniel and Michael Chmel. *The Quality Revolution and Health Care.* Milwaukee: ASQC Quality Press, 1991.

Smith, Frederick. "The Human Side of Quality." Address to the ASQC National Quality Forum, October 1990.

Spechler, Jay W. *When America Does It Right: Case Studies in Service Quality.* Norcross, Ga.: Industrial Engineering and Management Press, 1988.

Tice, Lou. "Investments in Excellence." Videotape. Seattle: The Pacific Institute, 1986.

Tice, Lou. "Strategic Thinking, Strategic Planning." Videotape. Seattle: The Pacific Institute, 1988.

U.S. Department of Commerce. "Baldrige Award Application." Washington, D.C., 1990.

U.S. Department of Education. "America 2000: An Education Strategy." Washington, D.C., 1991.

Walton, Mary. *The Deming Management Method.* New York: Perigree Books, Putnam, 1986.

Index